Post-Impressionism

Cross-Currents in
European and American Painting

1880–1906

19 Cézanne *Mont Sainte-Victoire*

*This exhibition was made possible
by a generous grant from
General Telephone & Electronics Corporation*

Post-Impressionism

Cross-Currents in
European and American Painting

1880–1906

National Gallery of Art
Washington
1980

Photographic Credits

This catalogue was produced by the Editors Office, National Gallery of Art, Washington. Printed by Princeton Polychrome Press, Princeton, New Jersey. The type is Melior, set by Composition Systems Inc., Arlington, Virginia. The text paper is Warren Lustro Offset Enamel Dull. Designed by Frances P. Smyth

Second edition, revised

Exhibition dates at the National Gallery of Art
May 25-September 1, 1980

Front cover: Paul Gauguin, *Contes barbares* (detail)
Folkwang Museum, Essen
Back cover: Georges Seurat, *Lighthouse at Honfleur* (detail)
Collection Mr. and Mrs. Paul Mellon
Frontispiece: Paul Cézanne, *Mont Sainte-Victoire,*
Collection Walter H. Annenberg

Library of Congress Cataloging in Publication Data

Main entry under title:

Post-impressionism.

   Catalog for an exhibition held at the National Gallery of Art, Washington, May 25-Sept. 1, 1980.
   1. Post-impressionism (Art)—Exhibitions.
I. United States. National Gallery of Art.
ND192.P6P66   759.05'6'0740153   80-13795

Save for those listed below, all the photographs appearing in this catalogue were provided by the lenders to the exhibition, who are noted in each entry. For their assistance and cooperation we are most grateful.

ACL, Brussels, cat. no. 240
Agraci, cat. no. 113
Jörg P. Anders, Berlin, cat. no. 178
Annan, Glasgow, cat. no. 44
Hallam Ashley, cat. no. 202
Attilio, Bacci, cat. no. 226
Bérard, cat. no. 153
Foto Brunel, Lugano, cat. nos. 187, 188
Bulloz, Paris, cat. nos. 2, 103, 164
H. Cooper & Son, Northampton, cat. no. 209
Prudence Cumming Associates (color), cat. nos. 5, 8, 23, 33, 34, 52, 54, 57, 96, 109, 145, 158, 174, 205, 206, 216, 224, 236
Walter Dräyer, Zurich, cat. nos. 14, 20, 64, 205
Alberto Flammer, Locarno, cat. no. 45
Foto-Hinz SWB, Allschwil, cat. no. 53
David A. Fry, cat. no. 252
Giraudon, Paris, cat. nos. 102, 114, 115, 160
Helga Photo Studio Inc., New York, cat. no. 104
G. Howald, Bern, cat. no. 131
Gerald Kraus, cat. no. 270
Landesbildstelle, Berlin, cat. no. 189
Charles P. Mills & Son, Philadelphia, cat. nos. 15, 74, 118
Otto E. Nelson, New York, cat. nos. 30, 158
Mario Perotti, Milan, cat. no. 215
Photo d'Art, Speltdoorn, cat. no. 231
Photo Studios Limited, London, cat. no. 8
Eric Pollitzer, cat. nos. 17, 156
David Preston, cat. no. 262
Rheinisches Bildarchiv, Cologne, cat. no. 183
Marcus Roberts Studios, Eastbourne, cat. no. 232
John D. Schiff, New York, cat. no. 87
Schmolz-Huth, Cologne, cat. no. 49
Service de Documentation Photographique de la Réunion des Musées Nationaux, Paris, cat. nos. 39, 95, 100, 112, 213
Service Photographique du Musée National d'Art Moderne—Centre National d'Art et de Culture Georges Pompidou, Paris, cat. no. 154
Taylor & Dull, Inc., New York, cat. no. 271
Charles Uht, New York, cat. no. 108
West Park Studios, Leeds, cat. no. 105
Wintex Limited, London, cat. no. 199

Contents

6   *Foreword*
J. CARTER BROWN

9   *Lenders to the Exhibition*

11   *Introduction*
ALAN BOWNESS

13   *Notes to Users*

15   *France*
JOHN HOUSE AND MARYANNE STEVENS

153   *Germany, Norway, and Switzerland*
GILLIAN PERRY

169   *Great Britain*
ANNA GRUETZNER

187   *Italy*
SANDRA BERRESFORD

203   *The Low Countries*
MARYANNE STEVENS

219   *The United States*
WANDA CORN AND JOHN WILMERDING

241   *Chronology*

244   *Select Bibliography*

247   *Acknowledgments*

248   *Index of Artists*

72 van Gogh *Tarascon Coaches*

Foreword

This exhibition is at once a celebration and an exploration. The towering masters of post-impressionism, most notably Cézanne, van Gogh, Gauguin, and Seurat, are among the most beloved artists in the entire canon of western painting. Fortunately, they are well represented in many American museums. Less seen by the public are the fabulous holdings in private collections and in the more out-of-the-way public collections abroad. To have the opportunity to gather together some of the major achievements of these four artists from all these sources would in itself be cause for rejoicing.

In addition to this, however, the National Gallery has the opportunity to present this summer an exhibition that goes far beyond this limited selection. So dazzled have we become by the achievements of the major figures working in France that we have tended to scant the complex and fascinating context of artistic experimentation that characterizes this fecund period, not only in France but in countries across Europe and in the United States.

This exhibition, shown initially in England, is the first in which that context has been so comprehensively examined. Alan Bowness, formerly professor of art history at the Courtauld Institute, University of London, and recently appointed Director of the Tate Gallery, has served as chairman of a selection committee made up of a team of young British scholars whose freshness of eye and depth of knowledge have brought new insights into our understanding of this period.

The exhibition held at the Royal Academy in the winter of 1979–1980, with the slightly different title, *Post-Impressionism, Cross-Currents in European Painting*, has served as the basis for the present show. For the American version, however, the size of the exhibition has been reduced by almost a third; the focus sharpened, with a greater concentration on a smaller number of artists; the span of the show precisely defined between 1880 and 1906, the year of Cézanne's death; and an American section added. It had been, in fact, the original intention of the organizers to include the work of American artists, and they were delighted when the Gallery offered its curator of American painting, John Wilmerding, who collaborated with Professor Wanda Corn to select this additional section and write the texts accompanying it.

The original catalogue, a model of its kind, has already become an art-historical reference work; this present publication records the show in its new form, with an abbreviated version of the original introduction, brief essays for each country and biographical sketches for each artist.

Rare indeed is the opportunity for a museum to rework an exhibition already assembled and hanging. The London scholars all had fresh ideas as a result of seeing the paintings in the initial show in juxtaposition. With the constraints of a smaller exhibition space in Washington, and the opportunity to borrow some pictures this summer that had not been available for the original showing, what has emerged is in essence a new exhibition, albeit one with a very strong resemblance to its parent.

Normally art exhibitions are not put together in this way. They take years of planning, and the advantages presented here of being able to work from a show already in existence have been somewhat mitigated administratively by the excruciatingly tight schedule that has obtained in bringing this exhibition to the United States.

It was in late February, just weeks before the London show was to close, that we at the Gallery received definite word that the long-planned and large-scale exhibition from the Hermitage Museum in Leningrad would not take place in the East Building in May. When we broached the idea of filling its place with the *Post-Impressionist* show, Norman Rosenthal, the secretary of the exhibition at the Royal Academy, quite visibly blanched, but manfully pledged on the spot to bend every effort to help us bring this about.

Unlike exhibitions that come from one museum or represent the collection of one lender, this show involves pictures from no fewer than 185 different sources. Each loan had to be negotiated separately; packing, conservation, shipping, escort, and insurance matters carefully worked out; and a new catalogue prepared on very short notice.

In this complex undertaking we cannot speak too highly of the efforts of Mr. Rosenthal, the London organizers, and the Gallery staff. In particular we must thank Lyndel King, coordinator for the exhibition, who was generously lent to us by Control Data Corporation of Minneapolis, which had been the corporate sponsor for the Hermitage show. To Sir Hugh Casson and Frederick Gore of the Royal Academy as well as Mr. Rosenthal and his able assistant, Jane Hepburne-Scott, and to Alan Bowness, John House, MaryAnne Stevens, Sandra Berresford, Anna Gruetzner, and Gillian Perry go our warmest thanks. MaryAnne Stevens and John House, as codirectors of the original exhibition, were particularly helpful in the selection of the revised show, and Mr. House accomplished a prodigious feat in bringing the text of the new catalogue together within the available time.

An undertaking of this magnitude in this day of skyrocketing costs is not an inexpensive proposition. The National Gallery by statute cannot charge admission, and we are therefore particularly grateful to General Telephone & Electronics Corporation, especially Theodore F. Brophy, chairman and chief executive officer, and Alfred C. Viebranz, senior vice president of that organization, whose generous grant has made this showing possible.

The exhibition has also been financed through the Gallery's federal appropriations, which include funds specifically designated for our special exhibitions program. For their continuing faith in this activity, we are appreciative of the sympathetic interest of the Office of Management and Budget, the Appropriations Subcommittee on the Department of the Interior and Related Agencies of the House of Representatives, especially its chairman, Congressman Sidney R. Yates of Illinois, and, on the Senate side, the corresponding committee, chaired by Senator Robert C. Byrd of West Virginia.

Gallery staff involved in mounting this exhibition are too numerous to list here, but we would like to mention in particular the extraordinary efforts of several people, including Peter Davidock, registrar, Gaillard Ravenel and Mark Leithauser, who designed the exhibition, Frances Smyth and Cathy Gebhard, who put together the catalogue for the Gallery, William J. Williams, who planned the educational materials, Carol Kelley, who organized the secretarial effort, as well as all the hardworking people in their departments and the other concerned staff of this institution.

Finally, and most importantly, it is the lenders to this show to whom we are immeasurably indebted. A list of them appears on the following page, although many have asked to remain anonymous. Their collective faith in this fertile period of the history of western art is amply evidenced by this exhibition in which all of us here at the National Gallery feel privileged to have taken part.

J. Carter Brown
Director

Lenders to the Exhibition

Julian J. Aberbach
Aberdeen Art Gallery, Scotland
Albright-Knox Art Gallery, Buffalo
Arthur G. Altschul
Mr. Walter H. Annenberg
Art Institute of Chicago
The Visitors of the Ashmolean
    Museum, Oxford, England
The Baltimore Museum of Art
Mrs. Anthony Bamford
Barber Institute of Fine Arts, Uni-
    versity of Birmingham, England
Bayerische Staatsgemälde-
    sammlungen, Munich
Jean Claude Bellier
The City of Bristol Museum and
    Art Gallery, England
Brücke-Museum, Berlin
Canajoharie Library and Art Gal-
    lery, New York
Museum of Art, Carnegie Institute,
    Pittsburgh
Castle Museum of Art, Archaeology and
    Natural History, Norwich, England
Civica Galleria d'Arte Moderna, Milan
Civica Galleria d'Arte Moderna, Turin
Civico Museo Antonio Borgogna,
    Vercelli, Italy
Sterling and Francine Clark Art
    Institute, Williamstown,
    Massachusetts
The Estate of Sir Charles Clore
Courtauld Institute Galleries, London
Mrs. Joan Crowell
J. F. Denis, France
The Denver Art Museum
Detroit Institute of Arts
Mrs. Pamela Diamand
Collection Durand-Ruel
M. Feilchenfeldt, Zurich
The Fine Arts Museums of San
    Francisco
Mr. and Mrs. Robert Fitzmaurice
Flint Institute of Arts, Michigan
Louis Franck, Chalet Arno, Gstaad
Galleria d'Arte Moderna, Venice
Galleria Nazionale d'Arte
    Moderna, Rome
Mr. and Mrs. Jacques Gelman,
    Mexico City
Gesellschaft Kruppsche
    Gemäldesammlung, Essen
Gimpel Family Collection
Glasgow Art Gallery and Museum
Mrs. Samuel Godfrey
Basil Goulandris, Lausanne
Mrs. Florence Gould, U.S.A.
Graves Art Gallery, Sheffield, England
Guildhall Art Gallery, London
Calouste Gulbenkian Foundation,
    Lisbon

W. Averell Harriman Collection
The High Museum of Art, Atlanta
Hirshhorn Museum and Sculpture
    Garden, Smithsonian
    Institution, Washington
Hunterian Art Gallery, University
    of Glasgow
John G. Johnson Collection,
    Philadelphia
Josefowitz Collection, Switzerland
Bernhard Kaufmann, Haus am
    Weyerberg, Worpswede
Kimbell Art Museum, Fort Worth, Texas
Koninklijk Museum voor Schone
    Kunsten, Antwerp, Belgium
Kunsthalle, Bremen
Kunsthalle, Hamburg
Kunsthaus, Zurich
Kunstmuseum, Basel
Kunstmuseum, Bern
Laing Art Gallery, Newcastle-
    upon-Tyne, England
Leeds City Art Galleries, England
Mr. and Mrs. Alexander Lewyt
Ludwig Museum, Cologne
Sir Jack Lyons, CBE
Marcel Mabille, Brussels
Morton D. May
Henry P. McIlhenny
Mr. and Mrs. Paul Mellon
Memorial Art Gallery of the Uni-
    versity of Rochester, New York
The Metropolitan Museum of Art,
    New York
Musée de l'Annonciade, Saint-Tropez
Musée des Beaux-Arts Jules
    Chéret, Nice
Musée des Beaux-Arts, Liège
Musée des Beaux-Arts, Orléans
Musée des Beaux-Arts de Rennes
Musée Gustave Moreau, Paris
Musée du Haubergier, Senlis
Musée du Louvre, Paris
Musée Matisse, Cimiez, Nice
Musée Municipal des Beaux-Arts,
    Quimper
Musée Nationale d'Art Moderne—
    Centre Georges Pompidou, Paris
Musée d'Orsay, Paris
Musée du Petit Palais, Paris
Musée du Prieuré, St. Germain-en-Laye
Musée Saint-Denis, Reims
Musées Royaux des Beaux-Arts de
    Belgique, Brussels
Museo Nazionale della Scienza e
    Tecnica, Milan
Museum Boymans-van Beuningen,
    Rotterdam
Museum of Fine Arts, Boston
Museum Folkwang, Essen

The Museum of Modern Art, New York
Nasjonalgalleriet, Oslo
Staatliche Museen Preussischer
    Kulturbesitz, Nationalgalerie, Berlin
Trustees of the National Gallery, London
National Gallery of Canada, Ottawa
National Gallery of Ireland, Dublin
National Gallery of Scotland, Edinburgh
National Museum of Wales, Cardiff
National Portrait Gallery, London
Nelson Gallery—Atkins Museum,
    Kansas City, Missouri
Niedersächsisches Landes-
    museum, Hanover
Northampton Art Gallery, England
Oakland Museum, California
Art Gallery of Ontario, Toronto
William S. Paley
The Parrish Art Museum, South-
    ampton, New York
Henry and Rose Pearlman
    Foundation, Inc.
M. Michel Perinet, Paris
Petit Palais, Geneva
Philadelphia Museum of Art
The Phillips Collection, Washington
Mr. and Mrs. Gifford Phillips
Museum of Art, Rhode Island
    School of Design, Providence
Rijksmuseum Kröller-Müller,
    Otterlo, The Netherlands
Rijksmuseum Vincent Van Gogh,
    Amsterdam
Rochdale Art Gallery, England
Guy Roussel
The St. Louis Art Museum
Ludwig Roselius Sammlung, Bremen
Santa Barbara Museum of Art,
    California
Mrs. Bertram Smith, New York
Southampton Art Gallery, England
Sam Spiegel
Rodolphe Staechelin Foundation, Basel
Stedelijk Museum, Amsterdam
Mr. and Mrs. George Szpiro, London
The Trustees of the Tate Gallery, London
Thyssen-Bornemisza Collection,
    Lugano-Castagnola, Switzerland
The Toledo Museum of Art, Ohio
The Victoria and Albert Museum,
    London
Wadsworth Atheneum, Hartford,
    Connecticut
Mr. and Mrs. Robert Walker
Wallraf-Richartz Museum, Cologne
Mr. and Mrs. John Hay Whitney
The Whitney Museum of
    American Art, New York
Mrs. Norman B. Woolworth, New York

56   Gauguin   *Sunflowers and Apples*

Introduction

ALAN BOWNESS

The term "post-impressionist" was coined by the English critic Roger Fry in 1910. Seeking a title for an exhibition of modern French art, in which he aimed to signal the demise of impressionism, he chose what he called the "somewhat negative label" of post-impressionist as an umbrella to cover the diverse artists whose work he was presenting. With the title, *Manet and the Post-Impressionists*, the show opened at the Grafton Galleries in London on 8 November 1910. Its three principal artists were Paul Gauguin, Vincent van Gogh, and Paul Cézanne; Manet was introduced as their precursor in the search for ways out of the cul-de-sac of naturalism.

In his preface to the exhibition catalogue, entitled "The Post-Impressionists," Fry defined what he saw as the characteristics of this new school of painting:

In no school does individual temperament count for more. In fact, it is the boast of those who believe in this school, that its methods enable the individuality of the artist to find completer self-expression in his work than is possible to those who have committed themselves to representing objects more literally . . . the Post-Impressionists consider the Impressionists too naturalistic.

Fry realized the great differences between his three principal artists, emphasizing the structural qualities of Cézanne's art, van Gogh's emotionalism, and Gauguin's concern with the power of abstract form. Georges Seurat found only a small part in this show, alongside younger painters who included Henri Matisse and Pablo Picasso. Only paintings from France were exhibited, but in his preface Fry pointed out that this new movement had already found disciples all over Europe and in America.

The idea of post-impressionism, then, was born after its principal protagonists were dead; unlike most of the labels which characterize modern art movements, it was neither deliberately coined nor reluctantly accepted by the artists themselves. Since Fry's first exhibition, the expression's terms of reference have widened. Fry himself later realized that he had been wrong to exclude Seurat from his post-impressionist pantheon, coming to see Seurat's neo-impressionism as an integral part of the artistic developments of the period. In subsequent discussions, the term has gained general acceptance as a useful description of the phase in French painting which occurred between 1880 and 1906 and of this phase's immediate impact on the art of other countries.

The present exhibition spreads the post-impressionist net wider than before, broadening the context in which we place the paintings of Cézanne, Gauguin, van Gogh, and Seurat. That crucial change of direction in the 1880s, the shift from appearance to experience as the justification for art, did not involve the great post-impressionist masters alone. This crisis of direction was also experienced by the principal painters of the impressionist group—themselves in an important sense post-impressionists in their later work. Other painters of the time, too, shared the same general concerns, both the lesser known associates of the great artists, and the more conservative painters who exhibited their work in the annual Salons. This exhibition includes a number of paintings by these innovative Salon artists, demonstrating their stylistic experiments and novel interpretations of subject matter, which distinguish their work from that of the more conventional Salon painter.

Painters outside France also participated in this quest for a type of painting which went beyond naturalism. In each country, the pattern was revealingly different; artists from varied social and cultural backgrounds evolved their own alternatives to direct representational painting, sometimes looking to the French for their solutions, but at other times deliberately working within their own national traditions. The reactions of younger artists are another important facet of the period. However, the exhibition concludes in 1906, with the flowering of fauvism in the art of Matisse and Derain. The emergence of cubism in the art of Picasso and Braque from 1907 onward introduced a range of new issues beyond the scope of the present show.

Looking back after almost a hundred years, we still regard the art of Cézanne, Gauguin, van Gogh, and Seurat as an apogee in the history of art, a moment when a high point was reached with a conjunction of stars of a magnitude and illumination unlikely to be seen together again for a very long time. The present exhibition by placing these stars in context will add immeasurably to our understanding and appreciation of their brilliance.

Notes to Users

While the works of art in the exhibition are presented
both thematically and by country, the catalogue
is divided into geographical sections.
Within each section, artists appear in the
chronological order of their birth. A few artists are
listed not under the country of their birth, but where
their importance for the exhibition lies—van Gogh,
Meyer de Haan, and Vallotton all appear under France.
An alphabetical index of all the artists included in the
exhibition appears at the end of this catalogue, as do a
chronology and selected bibliography.

Within the catalogue entries on each artist, the
paintings are listed in chronological order, after a brief
note on the artist's life and historical importance.
Where possible, pictures are given the title by which
they were originally exhibited and otherwise that by
which they are best known.

A simple date, after the title, indicates that the picture
was definitely executed or, if painted over a span of
years, completed during this year. A date preceded by
"c." is approximate. Two dates separated by an oblique
stroke indicate that the picture was definitely
executed within this span of years.

Inscriptions on the picture are transcribed in full,
where possible, with their nature and placement
indicated by the following abbreviations:

s   —signed
ns   —not signed
d   —dated
b   —bottom
t   —top
l   —left
c   —center
r   —right
insc—inscribed
rev —reverse

All works are oil on canvas, unless otherwise stated.
Sizes are given to the nearest 0.5 cm. and to the
nearest ¼ in.; height precedes width.

The notation "R.A. no." indicates that the painting
was exhibited, under that number, in the version of the
present exhibition held at the Royal Academy of Arts,
London, 1979–1980; full documentary and analytical
entries for all these works appear in the catalogue to
that exhibition, *Post-Impressionism, Cross-Currents in
European Painting*.

54
Gauguin
Annah the Javanese

France

JOHN HOUSE AND MARYANNE STEVENS

By the year 1880 the painters of the impressionist group had reached an apparent impasse. In the 1870s, they had mastered the art of sketching from nature, of translating their visual experience into rapid, often bold brushstrokes which conveyed the immediacy of their vision. However, critics continued to censure them for the neglect of organized form and serious content in their paintings, and at the same time the impressionist painters themselves began to wonder whether naturalism, in itself, was an adequate goal, whether it could make a complete and serious art. Each of the impressionists, in different ways, later tried to reintroduce more permanent values into his paintings, to go beyond naturalism.

In the same years, other artists in France came to reject all that impressionism had stood for. There had been, throughout the nineteenth century, a tradition of idealistic and imaginative painting, and in the later 1880s a number of painters turned back to this tradition, emphasizing the primary role of the artist's creative imagination and seeking to convey in paint "the idea," rather than the confused appearances of the visible world.

In these two points of view, we find the focus of artistic debate in France in the last years of the nineteenth century: should the artist take nature as his starting point, or should he create a new reality from his imagination? This question had crucial consequences both for the artist's working methods and for his subject matter. In his technique, should he use the variety of nature's forms and textures as the basis for his interpretations, or should he turn his back on outdoor painting and impose a studio-based order and unity on his methods? And in his choice of subject, should particular sites and specific occasions supply his raw material, or could he feel free to create new subjects, combining as he pleased elements from nature and from his imagination?

The history of post-impressionism in France is, in a sense, the history of the different answers which painters found to these questions. The later paintings of the impressionists themselves are an essential part of the story, as is the work of the younger artists who rejected impressionism completely. Simultaneously, the same issues came to preoccupy many conventional painters who continued to exhibit their work at the annual Salons. The diversity of their responses was as rich as that of the avant-garde. Learning from the impressionists, these Salon painters explored more heightened colors and looser techniques; they also

fig. 1   Gauguin. *Vision after the Sermon*. National Gallery of Scotland, Edinburgh

sought out novel subject matter, as exemplified by the environmental portraits of Besnard. Yet, the solutions of all these artists do have one essential factor in common: they seek to give the viewer a more active role, involving him by empathy in the painter's experience, instead of making him merely a witness to the painter's dialogue with nature.

From the diversity of painting during the period, three main threads emerge, three basic ways in which painters sought to enrich the form and meaning of their work: by pursuing pictorial unity, by emphasizing the expressive value of their subjects, and by seeking "abstraction." Pictorial unity was a central aim for Cézanne, expression for van Gogh, and abstraction for Gauguin. None of these categories is a rigid one, and they do not exclude each other; but they help to illuminate the main patterns of development in the period.

Cézanne, for example, continued to paint his landscapes from nature, but he increasingly emphasized the importance of the internal organization of the picture, of its forms, its colors, and its brushwork. He attempted to suggest form and space by the relationship of colored planes on the surface of the canvas, arranged so that the viewer would sense continuous rhymes of pattern and color running throughout the picture. This coherence of treatment was his way of expressing the unity which he felt underlying all natural scenes.

Cézanne's unity is predominantly one of structure, whereas other painters sought unity in atmospheric effects. Claude Monet concentrated on the nuances of sunlight and mists, translated into rich harmonies of colors in the series of canvases which he painted after 1890. Seurat, too, wanted to recreate the effects of nature in terms of a colored harmony, but he evolved a quite different technique from Monet's to achieve this, using juxtaposed points of clear color, whose vibrations suggest the shimmer of light. This style was christened neo-impressionism.

In the 1880s, Monet had expanded his treatment of nature in a rather different direction, seeking extreme effects—dramatic storms, dazzling Mediterranean sun—and treating them with dynamic brushwork and rich color contrasts. Van Gogh adopted the idea of using an accentuated technique to express the meanings of nature, but unlike Monet he was more interested in its underlying patterns and cycles—the seasons, night and day, life and death—than its surface appearances. His vigorous, flowing brushwork was used to suggest these vital forces, while his color contrasts heightened the expressive effect of his subjects, both in his landscapes and in his figural scenes.

Van Gogh always felt the need to use natural inspiration as his starting point, in strong contrast to Gauguin, who from 1888 onward insisted on the primacy of the artistic imagination, rejecting direct painting from nature. Both men wanted their paintings to convey the fuller meaning of their subjects, but, in contrast to van Gogh's impulsive handling, Gauguin simplified and flattened his forms to extract the essence of his subjects by emphasizing their decorative rhythms, by "abstracting" them, as he put it. In Brittany he stressed the stark contours of the landscape and the primitive customs and costumes of the people, seen in *Vision after the Sermon* of 1888 (fig. 1); after 1891, in the South Seas, he combined native figures with more timeless themes of good and evil, often borrowing poses from past art, to increase the suggestive effect of his scenes.

The roots of Gauguin's artistic theories were literary as much as pictorial. The aims of literary symbolism, codified in two manifestos in 1886, were to reject naturalistic subject matter and the direct imitation of the visible world and to seek instead to express "the idea," the inner mental experience. These goals were taken up by Louis Anquetin and Emile Bernard in 1886-1887. Such new subject matter demanded new artistic forms, inspiring the invention of the style which they called cloisonnism, whose crisp outlines and flat color planes rejected nature and impressionism in order to evoke mood. Gauguin was formulating similarly antinaturalistic ideas at the same time, and he learned from Bernard's simplified style when the two men worked together in Brittany in 1888, as seen in *Vision after the Sermon*.

At times, Gauguin adopted more overtly mystical and allegorical themes, which bring him nearer to a different branch of symbolist thought in France, to theorists who advocated detailed allegorical programs applied to timeless, esoteric themes. The Rosicrucian theories of Sâr Péladan, who mounted the exhibitions of the Salon de la Rose + Croix of 1892-1897, belong to this branch. The discussion of symbolist painting as a whole, and of its relationship with post-impressionism, has been clouded by a failure to distinguish clearly between allegorical symbolism and that which uses everyday objects and effects to evoke more general levels of meaning. This latter type of symbolism, pioneered by the poet Stéphane Mallarmé, is central to an understanding of post-impressionism. In these paintings new ways of organizing form and color were evolved as a means of conveying a fuller sense of the significance of the painter's subjects. The treatment of forms was seen as inseparable from their meaning, and this meaning was evoked purely by the organization of the forms and colors on the canvas, rather than depending on a literal description of objects in the visible world.

In an essay of 1890, Maurice Denis emphasized the primacy of formal values in the work of art: "Remember that a painting—before being a battle-horse, a nude woman, or some little genre scene—is

fig. 2 Seurat. *A Sunday Afternoon on the Ile de la Grande Jatte*. Courtesy of the Art Institute of Chicago, Helen Birch Bartlett Memorial Collection

essentially a flat surface covered with colors arranged in a certain order." However, the post-impressionists' concentration on developing new pictorial language was integrally linked to the way they conceived their subject matter. Their favorite themes lent themselves to many different interpretations. Landscape remained a prime subject.

For Cézanne and Monet, it was essentially unpeopled: unified by its structure for Cézanne, by its atmospheric effects for Monet. But many artists felt that landscape only gained a full meaning when it mirrored the experiences of the people who lived in it. Camille Pissarro aimed to express the "true poem of the countryside" by showing peasants working in harmony with the land, as an expression of his anarchistic beliefs in the value of unstructured agrarian communities. For van Gogh, on the other hand, it was the cycles of life which expressed man's underlying relationship with nature.

The landscapes of Brittany, a comparatively primitive region of France, where men and women depended on the earth and the sea for a livelihood, appealed to many artists who were seeking an expressive natural subject. Gauguin wanted his Breton scenes to reflect the muted, yet powerful note which he found there; similarly, the harshness of Breton life became a central theme for painters like Charles Cottet and Lucien Simon in the 1890s. The religious customs of Brittany also gave artists the chance of introducing a level of spiritual meaning into their paintings without resorting to abstruse mysticism; on occasions, though, as in the work of Gauguin, such themes became the vehicle for more private statements about the artist's own experience and about his relationship with society.

Although Gauguin repudiated the values of western society in his search for the primitive in Brittany and the South Seas, other painters found modern life a rich source of inspiration. The modern urban scene had been interpreted by the impressionists in the 1860s and 1870s in a mood of studied detachment, but themes of city life were taken up again in the 1880s in a rather different manner, emphasizing social concerns and the artificiality of the fashionable scene. Seurat's major paintings of urban recreation, such as *Sunday on the Ile de la Grande Jatte* (fig. 2), express this artificiality by stiff, stylized drawing. Both he and Henri de Toulouse-Lautrec painted Parisian entertainments: Seurat with an ironic sense of their false gaiety, Lautrec with a rich and humane understanding of their glamour and its attendant suffering.

The contrast between modern and mystical themes emerges most clearly in the paintings of the nabis. They were inspired to form an artistic group by Paul Sérusier's *The Talisman* (cat. no. 115), a radically simplified, antinaturalistic landscape painted under Gauguin's instructions in Brittany, and their ideas were formulated by Maurice Denis in his essay of 1890, "Définition du néo-traditionnisme." The nabis shared a desire to find a decorative nonnaturalistic style of painting, but Denis and Sérusier favored religious themes, while Edouard Vuillard and Pierre Bonnard selected subjects from modern Paris. Sérusier was inspired by the primitivism of Brittany, Denis by fifteenth-century Italian art, but both attempted to give new life to the tradition of mystical painting. Vuillard and Bonnard also wanted to evoke emotions but derived them from everyday life; Vuillard, in particular, used the patterning of his domestic interiors to express the psychological and emotional states underlying everyday domestic experience.

Despite such diverse subjects and different pictorial styles, post-impressionist painters in France had a number of common concerns: they felt that painting had to go beyond mere naturalism; they wanted their art to involve the viewer in a more active way; and they felt that the message of their paintings should be expressed not only by subject matter but also by formal language. Their pictorial styles developed as ways of expressing the meaning of their art. In exploring the relationships between style and content, the painters of the post-impressionist period were able to realize Cézanne's declared aim, to make of impressionism "something solid and durable like the art of the museums."

Pierre Puvis de Chavannes   1824–1898

Although he belonged to an older generation, Puvis de
Chavannes' paintings, in which ideas were conveyed
by a dominant bounding line filled with flat
color, established him as a powerful influence on the
generation of the 1880s. Puvis was born in Lyon. He
visited Italy in 1847 and then studied in Paris where
he saw the recently completed murals by Théodore
Chassériau in the Cours des Comptes and decided to
devote his life to monumental mural decoration. This
ambition was fulfilled; during the rest of his life he
painted a series of highly acclaimed decorative
projects executed almost exclusively for public
buildings.

1   *Vision of Antiquity*   c. 1887/1888

Vision antique
sbl. P. Puvis de Chavannes
105 x 133 cm/41 1/4 x 52 1/4 in
Museum of Art, Carnegie Institute, Pittsburgh

Gustave Moreau   1826–1898

Like Puvis de Chavannes, Moreau belonged to an older generation of artists whose work had a profound influence upon young painters at the end of the nineteenth century. After studying in Paris under François Edouard Picot at the Ecole des Beaux-Arts, Moreau visited Italy in 1857–1859. On returning to Paris he combined the lessons of Leonardo da Vinci and Andrea Mantegna with those of his close friend, Chassériau. The exotic, often erotic subjects taken from classical, biblical, and literary sources, his rich, bejewelled paint surfaces, in which color has no descriptive function, existing purely for itself, and his position as a teacher at the Ecole des Beaux-Arts from 1892, all made Moreau a formative influence on such artists as Georges Rouault, Henri Evenepoel, and Matisse.

2   *The Sirens*   c. 1890

Les Sirènes
sbl. Gustave Moreau   93 x 62 cm/36 1/2 x 24 1/2 in
Musée Gustave Moreau, Paris
RA 145

5

Camille Pissarro 1830–1903

Born of Jewish parents in the West Indies, Pissarro moved to France in 1855. After studying briefly with Jean-Baptiste-Camille Corot in the late 1850s, he met the impressionists-to-be and became a leading figure in their group exhibitions of 1874–1886. He introduced Cézanne to landscape painting and worked with him regularly between 1872 and 1881. Pissarro painted mainly on a smallish scale, treating landscapes and peasant scenes. He adopted a tighter, more ordered style in c. 1877 and in 1886–1888 experimented with the neo-impressionist technique of Seurat, deciding subsequently that he found it too schematized and returning to a broader execution. His peasant scenes reflect his anarchistic beliefs in the possibility of a society based on small agrarian communities.

3 *Peasant Woman Digging* 1882

Paysanne bèchant
sdbl. C. Pissarro 82   65 x 54 cm/25 1/2 x 21 1/4 in
Collection Durand-Ruel
RA 152

4 *Ile Lacroix, Rouen, Effect of Fog* 1888

L'Ile Lacroix, Rouen, effet de brouillard
sdbr. C. Pissarro 1888   46.5 x 55 cm/18 1/4 x 21 3/4 in
John G. Johnson Collection, Philadelphia
RA 154

5 *Women Haymaking* 1889

Les Faneuses
sdbl. C. Pissarro 1889   65.5 x 81 cm/25 3/4 x 32 in
Kunstmuseum, Basel, Dr. H. C. Emile Dreyfus Foundation
RA 155 *(illustrated in color)*

3

4

Edouard Manet   1832–1883

After training with Thomas Couture then studying in
Italy, Manet returned to Paris where he lived until his
death. His paintings of modern life from the 1860s,
many of which were rejected from the Salon, won him
a central place among young artists. His freely painted
style owed much initially to the old masters, but after
1870 he was increasingly influenced by the open-air
work of the impressionists, particularly Monet.
However, for his major paintings he always
concentrated on figural subjects, and in his last works,

after 1880, he tried to go beyond naturalism in his
treatment of these themes and to convey more
suggestive moods, comparable to those sought by his
friend, the poet Mallarmé. These levels of meaning,
and his concern for formal values in his work, gave his
painting a fresh relevance for the generation of
younger artists reacting against impressionism.

6   *Spring (Jeanne)*   1881

   Le Printemps
   sdbl. Manet 1881   73 x 51 cm/28 3/4 x 20 in
   Private Collection

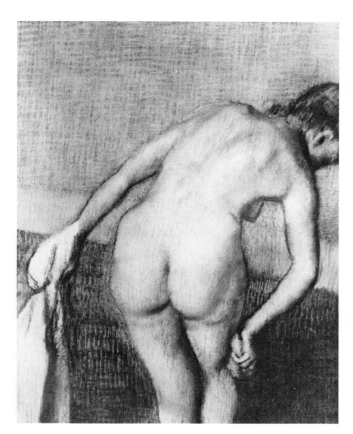

Edgar Degas 1834–1917

After an academic training from pupils of Jean-Auguste-Dominique Ingres and a period of study in Italy, Degas lived in Paris and, from the mid-1860s, concentrated on painting both portraits of friends and modern urban subjects—the ballet, café-concerts, racecourses, women working and bathing. He made important technical experiments, particularly with pastel, which he used increasingly after c. 1877 when his eyesight began to fail, giving this medium a new richness and density through superimposed layers of color. Although he exhibited with the impressionists, his methods were very different from theirs. His compositions, often asymmetrical and apparently disjointed, were carefully worked out from studies and were designed to express the unposed, natural appearance of a subject caught unawares.

7 *Woman Bathing* c. 1885

Femme prenant un tub
sbr. Degas   pastel   72 x 56 cm/28 1/4 x 22 in
Private Collection

8 *Portrait of Mademoiselle Hélène Rouart*   1886

Portrait de Mademoiselle Hélène Rouart
stamped br. Degas   161 x 120 cm/63 1/2 x 47 in
Gimpel Family Collection
RA 63 *(illustrated in color)*

9 *Dancers in Salmon-colored Skirts*   c. 1895

Danseuses, jupes saumon
stamped bl. Degas   pastel on paper
89 x 65 cm/35 x 25 1/2 in
Private Collection
RA 64

10

Henri Fantin-Latour   1836–1904

Having failed to gain admission to the Ecole des
Beaux-Arts, Fantin-Latour trained himself by copying
old masters in the Louvre and attending Gustave
Courbet's "Atelier du Réalisme" in 1861. Fantin is best
known for his group portraits and flower pieces
executed in a realistic style. However, he also had an
idealizing side to his art. His admiration for Eugène
Delacroix, together with close friendships in Parisian
avant-garde literary and musical circles, engendered
an interest in imaginary subjects, especially those
found in Richard Wagner's operas, which he depicted
in a technique indebted to Venetian sixteenth-century
masters, notably Titian.

11

10   *Immortality*   1889

   L'Immortalité
   sdbr. Fantin 89   117 x 87 cm/46 x 34 1/4 in
   National Museum of Wales, Cardiff
   RA 77

11   *Portrait of Sonia*   1890

   sdtr. A ma chére (sic) nièce Sonia/Fantin. 90
   109 x 81 cm/43 x 32 in
   National Gallery of Art, Washington,
   Chester Dale Collection

James Jacques Joseph Tissot   1836–1902

Born in Nantes, Tissot studied in Paris in the late
1850s, where he met Degas. In 1871, after involvement
in the Commune, he left Paris for London where he
lived until 1883. Here, he continued his interest in
themes from modern life, winning a reputation for
scenes of fashionable urban life. In 1885, he exhibited
a sequence of fifteen paintings of women in Paris,
which present the most characteristic female
occupations of the time, and in 1886 he began work on
a long sequence of biblical illustrations. His paintings,
freely brushed yet meticulous in detail, show
contemporary subjects in asymmetrical compositions
often reminiscent of Degas and Japanese prints.

12   *The Ladies of the Chariots*   1883/1885

Ces Dames de chars
sbr. J. J. Tissot   146 x 101 cm/57 1/2 x 39 3/4 in
Museum of Art, Rhode Island School of Design,
Providence, Gift of Walter Lowry
RA 218

Paul Cézanne   1839–1906

Cézanne came from Aix-en-Provence and always kept a home there, though he regularly visited Paris and northern France. In Paris in 1861 he met Camille Pissarro, who later introduced him to the impressionist circle and to landscape painting. He often painted with Pissarro up to 1881, when he also worked with Gauguin. Cézanne developed a style based on the modeling of forms by color, seeking to give landscape an order and solidity comparable with that of the old masters. He also painted portraits, peasant figures, and still lifes from nature and worked throughout his career on a sequence of imaginary figure compositions, the romantic subjects of his early years giving way by c. 1880 to monumental compositions of bathers. His work was known only to a narrow circle until 1895, when his paintings began to be exhibited more widely and came to have a vast influence on younger artists.

13   *Houses in Provence*   c. 1880

> ns. 65 x 81.5 cm/25 1/2 x 32 in
> National Gallery of Art, Washington,
> gift of Mr. and Mrs. Paul Mellon, 1973

14   *Still Life with Pots and Fruit*   1890/1894

> *Nature morte, pots et fruits*
> ns.   65 x 81.5 cm/25 3/4 x 32 in
> Private Collection
> RA 43

15 *The White Sugar Bowl* 1890/1894

Sucrier, poires et tapis
ns. 51 x 62 cm/20 x 24 1/2 in
Collection Henry P. McIlhenny

16 *Standing Nude* 1898/1899

Femme nue debout
ns. 92.5 x 71 cm/36 1/2 x 28 in
Anonymous Lender
RA 46

17 *The Bibémus Quarry* 1898/1900

La Carrière Bibémus
ns. 65 x 54 cm/25 1/2 x 21 1/4 in
Collection Sam Spiegel

19

18

18   *In the Park of the Château Noir*   c. 1902

Dans le parc du Château Noir
ns.   90.5 x 71.5 cm/35 3/4 x 28 1/4 in
Trustees of the National Gallery, London
RA 47

19   *Mont Sainte-Victoire*   1902/1906

La Montagne Sainte-Victoire
ns. 56.5 x 97 cm/22 1/4 x 38 1/4 in
Collection Walter H. Annenberg
(illustrated in color)

20   *Women Bathing*   1902/1906

Baigneuses
ns.   73.5 x 92.5 cm/29 x 36 1/2 in
Collection M. Feilchenfeldt, Zurich
RA 48

21 *Le Château Noir*   1900/1904

ns. 73.5 x 96.5 cm/29 x 38 in
National Gallery of Art, Washington,
Gift of Eugene and Agnes Meyer, 1958

Claude Monet   1840–1926

Introduced to landscape painting by Eugène Boudin
on the Channel coast in c. 1856, Monet met the future
impressionists in Paris in the 1860s. He was one of the
leading figures in the impressionist group exhibitions
from the 1870s. In the 1880s he traveled widely to
paint, but later turned increasingly to scenes around
Giverny in the Seine valley, where he moved in 1883
and built his water garden from 1892 onward. After
submitting large paintings to the Salon in the 1860s,
he favored smaller, more summarily treated
landscapes in the group shows from the 1870s; but
after 1880 he began to finish his canvases more fully,
emphasizing the patterns produced by his brushwork.
After 1890, in his series of paintings of single subjects

seen under different conditions, he focused on
recreating atmospheric effects in rich harmonies of
color.

22   *Pears and Grapes*   1880

Poires et raisins
sdtl. Claude Monet 1880   65 x 80 cm/25 1/2 x 31 1/2 in
Kunsthalle, Hamburg, West Germany
RA 135

23   *Varengeville Church*   1882

L'Eglise de Varengeville
sdbr. Claude Monet 82   65 x 81 cm/25 1/2 x 32 in
Barber Institute of Fine Arts, University of
Birmingham, England
RA 136   *(illustrated in color)*

24

25

24 *Storm on Belle-Isle 1886*

Tempête à Belle-Isle
sdbr. Claude Monet 86   60 x 73.5 cm/23 1/2 x 29 in
Private Collection, New York
RA 138

25 *Cap d'Antibes in the Mistral*   1888

Au Cap d'Antibes par vent de mistral
sdbl. Claude Monet 88   65 x 80 cm/25 1/2 x 31 1/2 in
Museum of Fine Arts, Boston,
Bequest of Arthur Tracy Cabot
RA 139

26   *Haystack in Winter*   1891

Meule, effet de neige, matin
sdbl. Claude Monet 91   65 x 92 cm/25 1/2 x 36 1/4 in
Museum of Fine Arts, Boston,
Gift of Misses Aimée and Rosamond Lamb in memory
of Mr. and Mrs. Horatio A. Lamb

27   *The Poplars, the Three Trees, Autumn*   1891

Les Peupliers, les trois arbres, automne
sdbr. Claude Monet 91   92 x 73.5 cm/36 1/4 x 29 in
Philadelphia Museum of Art, Gift of Chester Dale
RA 142

28 *Rouen Cathedral, West Façade*   1894

La Cathédrale de Rouen, le portail
sdbl. Claude Monet 94   100.5 x 66 cm/39 1/2 x 26 in
National Gallery of Art, Washington,
Chester Dale Collection

29 *Water Lilies*   1904

Nympheas
sdbr. Claude Monet 1904
87.5 x 91 cm/34 1/2 x 35 3/4 in
The Denver Art Museum,
Helen Dill Collection

30

Odilon Redon   1840–1916

After a lonely childhood on the family estate of
Peyrelebade outside Bordeaux, Redon went to Paris to
train first as an architect and then as a painter. After a
breakdown in c. 1864 he returned to Bordeaux where
he met the etcher Rodolphe Bresdin. Until 1879 Redon
worked almost exclusively in charcoal, amassing the
material for the 166 lithographs which he produced
between 1879 and 1899. Although he had always
painted, it was only in the mid-1890s that he began to
move toward the celebration of explosive color which
characterizes his work after 1900. Executed in pastel,
watercolor, and oils, these works relate to subjects
presented initially in charcoal and as lithographs, but,
unlike them, the later pictures have no captions and
express their inner meaning through color and surface
texture alone, so enabling them to escape the literary
interpretations given to the lithographs by symbolist
writers.

30   *Fallen Angel*   c. 1900

L'Ange déchu
sbr. Odilon Redon   81.5 x 100.5 cm/32 x 39 1/2 in
Collection Mrs. Bertram Smith, New York
RA 166

31   *Dream Shadows*   c. 1905

sbl. Odilon Redon   pastel on paper
49.5 x 63.5 cm/19 1/2 x 25 in
Collection Mrs. Joan Crowell
RA 169

33

31

32   *The Turquoise Vase*   c. 1905

Le Vase turquoise
sbr. Odilon Redon   65 x 50 cm/25 1/2 x 19 3/4 in
Private Collection, Switzerland
RA 167

33   *The Red Sphinx*   c. 1910

Le Sphinx rouge
sbr. Odilon Redon   61 x 50 cm/25 1/2 x 19 3/4 in
Private Collection, Switzerland
RA 170   *(illustrated in color)*

Pierre Auguste Renoir   1841–1919

Renoir lived for most of his life in Paris, until in 1902 he moved his base to the Riviera. He met the impressionists-to-be in the 1860s and showed in some of their group exhibitions, but also exhibited at the Salon during 1878–1883 when he was painting many fashionable portraits. His very spontaneous handling of the 1870s gave way, after a visit to Italy in 1881–1882, to a tighter, more linear execution, as he tried to reintroduce line and form into his art. At the same time, he turned to more timeless subjects, such as female nudes, in place of the scenes from modern life which he painted in the 1870s. Beginning in 1888, he adopted a looser technique, indebted to the French eighteenth century, in which he reintroduced freer brushwork without sacrificing the definition of form.

34   *Rocky Crags at L'Estaque*   1882

Rochers à l'Estaque
sdbl. Renoir 82   66 x 80.5 cm/26 x 31 3/4 in
Museum of Fine Arts, Boston,
Juliana Cheney Edwards Collection,
Bequest of Hannah Marcy Edwards in memory of her mother
RA 171

35   *La Roche-Guyon*   c. 1885

sbl. Renoir 47 x 56 cm/18 1/2 x 22 in
Aberdeen Art Gallery, Scotland
RA 172

36   *Young Girl Bathing*   1892

Baigneuse
sdbl. Renoir 92   81.5 x 65 cm/32 x 25 1/2 in
The Metropolitan Museum of Art, New York,
Robert Lehman Collection
RA 175

Alfred Guillou   1844–1926

Guillou was born in Brittany and trained in Paris at
the Ecole des Beaux-Arts. During the 1880s he
established his reputation as a painter of characteristic
Breton scenes. He was noted for the care with which
he recorded the rich traditions of a region as much
bound to its Celtic, pagan past as to the contemporary
realities of a precarious existence based largely upon
the sea and a rigid devotion to Roman Catholicism.

37   *The Arrival of the Pardon of St. Anne at
Fouesnant*   1887

L'Arrivée du Pardon de Ste Anne à Fouesnant
sbl. Alf. Guillou   281 x 216 cm/110 1/2 x 85 in
Musée Municipal des Beaux-Arts, Quimper, France
RA 108

Albert Maignan 1845–1908

Trained in Paris at the Ecole des Beaux-Arts, Maignan
made his Salon debut as a landscape painter. In 1868,
however, he embarked upon a highly acclaimed career
as a history painter which reached its apogee with the
exhibition of *Carpeaux* in 1892. Like other Salon
artists of the 1890s (e.g., Edmond Aman-Jean, Jean
Béraud, and Henri Martin), Maignan sought to reverse
the apparent decline in history painting by expressing
ideals through a combination of contemporary
references, naturalistic details, and philosophical
messages.

38   *The Passage of Fortune*   c. 1895

La Fortune passe
sbr. Albert Maignan   73 x 100 cm/28 3/4 x 39 1/4 in
Musée Saint-Denis, Reims, France
RA 120

Alfred Philippe Roll   1846–1919

Roll was born in Paris and lived there all his life. A
pupil of Jean Léon Gérôme, Léon Bonnat, and Henry
Joseph Harpignies, he first showed at the Salon in
1870 and won a first-class medal in 1877. His favored
subjects were portraits, scenes of modern life, and
idealized figures, all freely handled and based on a
close study of nature. In the 1880s and 1890s he
worked on a sequence of environmental figure
paintings of the typical characters of his age, each a
portrait of a named person, set in his normal working
context.

39   *Manda Lamétrie, Farmer's Wife*   1887

Manda Lamétrie, fermière
sdbl. Roll 87   214 x 161 cm/84 1/4 x 63 1/4 in
Musée du Louvre, Paris
RA 178

Jules Bastien-Lepage   1848–1884

Bastien-Lepage was born at Damvillers in northeastern
France and worked there for most of his career. He
studied at the Ecole des Beaux-Arts and won second
prize in the Prix de Rome competition in 1875. From
1878 onward, he made his reputation with a sequence
of paintings of peasant subjects. These are treated in
subdued color, with specific details picked out to
emphasize the mood of the scene. Bastien wanted to
go beyond simple naturalism and to express the poetry
which he found in nature. His work had a vast
influence in Europe and the United States in the
1880s.

40   *Poor Fauvette*   1881

Pauvre Fauvette
sdbl. and insc. J. Bastien-Lepage Damvillers 1881
162.5 x 125.5 cm/64 x 49 1/2 in
Glasgow Art Gallery and Museum
RA 10

Paul Gauguin   1848–1903

Gauguin was born in Paris, but lived in Peru from
1849 to 1855 and traveled widely before he took up a
career on the Paris stock exchange, where he lost his
job in 1883. He began to paint in c. 1873 and was
introduced to impressionism by Camille Pissarro. He
painted with Pissarro on occasion from 1879 and with
Cézanne in 1881. He visited Brittany regularly between
1886 and 1890, painted in Martinique in 1887, and
stayed at Arles with van Gogh in 1888. Gauguin
evolved an anti-impressionist style, which was
crystallized by his contact with Bernard in Brittany in
1888. He rejected direct painting from nature in favor
of working from his imagination and used flat,
decorative color planes to express a timeless, primitive
mood, often choosing overtly symbolic themes. He
lived in Tahiti during 1891–1893 and 1895–1901, before
moving to the Marquesas Islands. In the South Seas,
he combined local scenes with forms derived from
European and Oriental art to convey themes with more
generalized, suggestive meanings.

41   *Still Life with a Horse's Head*   c. 1886

> *Nature morte à la tête de cheval*
> sbr. Paul Gauguin 49 x 38 cm/19 1/4 x 15 in
> Private Collection, Switzerland
> RA 80

42   *The Breton Shepherdess*   1886

> *La Bergère bretonne*
> sdbl. P. Gauguin 86   61 x 73.5 cm/24 x 29 in
> Laing Art Gallery, Newcastle-upon-Tyne, England
> RA 81

43   *The Four Breton Women*   1886

Les Quatre bretonnes
sdbl. P. Gauguin 86   71 x 90 cm/28 x 35 1/2 in
Bayerische Staatsgemäldesammlungen, Munich,
West Germany
RA 82

44   *Martinique Landscape*   1887

Paysage de la Martinique
sdbr. P. Gauguin 87   115.5 x 89 cm/45 1/2 x 35 in
National Gallery of Scotland, Edinburgh
RA 83

45

47

47 *Still Life Fête Gloanec* 1888

Nature morte Fête Gloanec
d and insc br. Fête Gloanec Madeleine B 88
oil on canvas mounted on panel   38 x 53 cm/15 x 21 in
Musée des Beaux-Arts, Orléans, France
RA 85

48 *The Ham* 1889

Le Jambon
sbr (on table edge). P. Go
50 x 58 cm/ 19 3/4 x 22 3/4 in
The Phillips Collection, Washington

45 *Brittany Landscape with Swineherd* 1888

Paysage breton avec porcher
sdbr. P. Gauguin 88
73.5 x 92 cm/29 x 36 1/4 in
Anonymous Lender

46 *Laundresses at Arles* 1888

Les Lavandières à Arles
sdbl. P. Gauguin 1888
73 x 92 cm/28 3/4 x 36 1/4 in
Collection William S. Paley

46

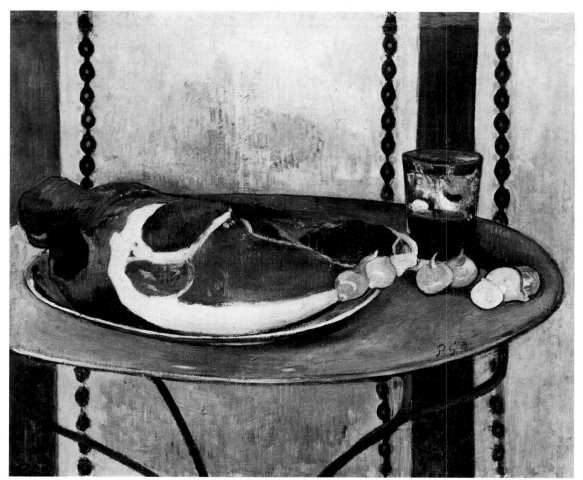

48

49   Naked Breton Boy   1889

Petit breton nu
sdbr. 89 P. Gauguin 93 x 73.5 cm/36 1/2 x 29 in
Wallraf-Richartz Museum, Cologne, West Germany
RA 88

50   Self-Portrait   1889

Autoportrait
sdbl. 1889./P Go   oil on panel
79 x 51.5 cm/31 1/4 x 20 1/4 in
National Gallery of Art, Washington,
Chester Dale Collection

51   *The Yellow Christ*   1889

Le Christ jaune
sdbr. P. Gauguin 89   92 x 73 cm/36 1/4 x 28 3/4 in
Albright-Knox Art Gallery, Buffalo, New York,
General Purchase Funds

52   *The Man with the Axe*   1891

L'Homme à la hache
sdbl. P. Gauguin 91   92 x 69 cm/36 1/4 x 27 1/4 in
Collection Mr. and Mrs. Alexander Lewyt
RA 89   *(illustrated in color)*

53   *When Will You Marry?*   1892

Nafea Faa ipoipo (Quand te maries-tu?)
sdbl. P. Gauguin 92; insc br. NAFEA Faa ipoipo
101.5 x 77.5 cm/40 x 30 1/2 in
Rodolphe Staechelin Foundation, Basel, Switzerland
RA 90

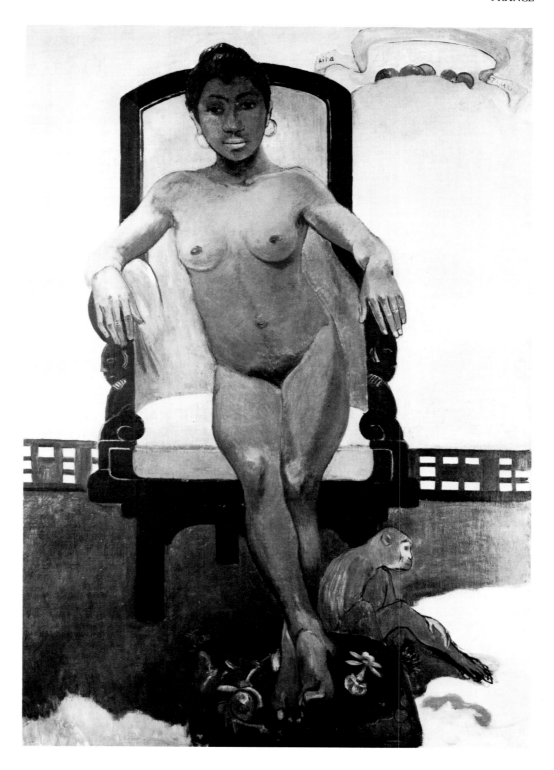

54   *Annah the Javanese*   1893/1894

Annah la Javanaise
ns; insc tr. AITA PARARI Tamari vahina Judith te
116 x 81.5 cm/45 3/4 x 32 in
Private Collection
RA 91   *(illustrated in color)*

55 *Christmas Night*
(The Blessing of the Oxen)   c. 1896?

Nuit de Noël (La Bénédiction des boeufs)
sbr. P. Gauguin   72 x 83 cm/28 1/4 x 32 3/4 in
Private Collection, Switzerland
RA 92

56 *Sunflowers and Apples* 1901

Tournesols et pommes
sdbl. P. Gauguin 1901
93 x 73 cm/36 1/2 x 28 3/4 in
Basil Goulandris, Lausanne, Switzerland
(illustrated in color)

57 *Contes barbares* 1902

sdbr and insc. Contes Barbares Paul Gauguin 1902
Marquises
131.5 x 90.5 cm/51 3/4 x 35 1/2 in
Museum Folkwang, Essen, West Germany
RA 93 *(illustrated in color)*

Jean Béraud   1849–1936

Born in Russia, Béraud trained under Bonnat at the
Ecole des Beaux-Arts and exhibited for the first time at
the Salon of 1873. He was a founding member of the
Société Nationale, with which he exhibited regularly
from 1890. Apart from successful portraits, Béraud
executed meticulous paintings of contemporary social
mores, scenes of the streets, and city entertainments of
the time. In response to the widespread religious
revival in art and literature during the 1890s, Béraud
applied his precise realism to biblical themes set in
modern dress, including recognizable notables of the
day; when exhibited at the Salon, these works
provoked great criticism as well as praise.

58   *Mary Magdalene in the House of the
Pharisee*   1891

La Madeleine chez le Pharisien
sdbr. Jean Béraud 1891   126.5 x 157 cm/50 x 61 3/4 in
Collection Mr. and Mrs. Robert Walker
RA 11

Paul Albert Besnard   1849–1934

Trained at the Ecole des Beaux-Arts in Paris, Besnard won acclaim at the Salon of 1880. In the 1880s, he developed a style based on a compromise between academic conventions and impressionist techniques, which he applied most dramatically in his large "environmental" society portraits. Rejecting both idealization and minute naturalism, the dominant tendencies in contemporary portraiture, he emphasized the sitters' surroundings, in order to reveal their personalities more fully, and, as he said, "to express their relationship with the world in which they live."

59   *Portrait of Mme. Roger Jourdain*   1886

Portrait de Mme. Roger Jourdain
sbl. A. Besnard   200 x 155 cm/78 3/4 x 61 in
Musée des Beaux-Arts Jules Chéret, Nice, France
RA 21

Eugène Carrière   1849–1906

Initially apprenticed to a lithographer in Strasbourg,
Carrière decided to become a painter in 1869 and went
to Paris to study at the Ecole des Beaux-Arts. He
visited London in 1876–1877 where he admired Joseph
Mallord William Turner's work. Toward the end of the
1880s his style moved away from somber naturalism to
a more expressive manner in which monochrome
mists envelop scenes of domestic interiors, portraits of
his family, and studies of mothers and children, and
endow them with a sense of mystery and
generalization which greatly appealed to the younger
generation of artists. He exchanged paintings with
Gauguin and executed portraits of Verlaine and
Edmond de Goncourt. In 1904 a banquet was given in
his honor, arranged by Auguste Rodin.

60   *Motherhood*   c. 1890

Maternité
sbl. Eugène Carrière   53.5 x 71 cm/21 x 28 in
National Museum of Wales, Cardiff
RA 37

Emile Schuffenecker 1851–1934

Although he could never afford to become a full-time painter, Schuffenecker played an important part in the artistic events of Paris during the 1880s. A colleague of Gauguin's at the stockbroking firm of Bertin, he encouraged Gauguin to take up painting, engineered his introduction to Camille Pissarro, and made his own home the Paris center for Gauguin's so-called School of Pont-Aven. He played a central role in the organization of the Café Volpini exhibition and gave Gauguin financial support before he left for Tahiti in 1891. Schuffenecker also made a significant contribution to the evolution of pictorial symbolism in c. 1888. He introduced Bernard to neo-impressionism in 1886, an event which led to Bernard's decision, following a visit to Paul Signac's studio, to reject all forms of impressionism for a style of painting in which "Ideas dominate the technique."

61 *Landscape—Two Cows in a Meadow* 1886

Deux vaches dans un pré
sdbl. Schuffenecker 1886
49 x 65 cm/19 1/4 x 25 1/2 in
Collection Mr. and Mrs. Robert Fitzmaurice
RA 184

Pascal Adolphe Jean
Dagnan-Bouveret 1852–1929

Dagnan-Bouveret entered Gérôme's atelier at the Ecole
des Beaux-Arts in 1869. Exhibiting regularly at the
Salon from 1876, he began to paint contemporary
subjects in a naturalistic style in 1879, possibly under
the influence of his friend, Bastien-Lepage. He
exhibited his first Breton theme at the Salon on 1887,
followed two years later by *Breton Women at a Pardon*
and a religious painting. This pair of paintings won
Dagnan-Bouveret grudging praise from Gauguin's
disciple, Denis, and set the tone for his work
throughout the 1890s. Apart from successful portraits
of Parisian aristocracy, religious paintings dominated
his late career.

62   *Breton Women at a Pardon*   1887

Bretonnes au pardon
sdbl. PAJ Dagnan-B 1887
125 x 141 cm/49 1/4 x 55 1/2 in
Calouste Gulbenkian Foundation, Lisbon
RA 58 *(not in exhibition)*

Jacob Meyer de Haan   1852–1895

Born into a well-to-do Amsterdam family of biscuit manufacturers, Meyer de Haan first worked in the family firm. By 1888, however, his enthusiasm for painting led him to Paris where he stayed with Théo van Gogh, met Vincent, and was introduced to Gauguin. He established a close relationship with Gauguin, working beside him in 1889 at Le Pouldu, adopting his style of schematic, patterned painting, and giving him financial support. Gauguin admired Meyer de Haan's artistic ability, as well as his intelligence and education. He painted two portraits of Meyer de Haan while he was alive in addition to one from memory, which can be seen on the left of *Contes barbares* (cat. no. 57).

63   *Le Pouldu*   1889

sdbl. and insc. Meyer de Haan Le Pouldu 1889
73.5 x 93 cm/29 x 36 3/4 in
Rijksmuseum Kröller-Müller, Otterlo, The Netherlands
RA 134

Vincent van Gogh   1853–1890

Son of a Dutch protestant minister, van Gogh tried various careers—the art trade, teaching, the ministry, and missionary work—before deciding to become a painter in c. 1880. He studied in The Hague in 1883 and in Antwerp during 1885–1886 before leaving for Paris, where he stayed for two years, learning from the impressionists and neo-impressionists and using brush and color with increasing boldness. He met Gauguin, Bernard, Signac, the Pissarros, and Toulouse-Lautrec, among others, before leaving for Arles, in Provence, in February 1888; Gauguin stayed with him there from October until van Gogh's breakdown in December 1888. Van Gogh lived in a hospital at Saint-Rémy near Arles in 1889–1890 and then moved to Auvers in northern France, where he killed himself. In his art, he presented nature through rich patterns and intense color-relationships, trying to extract its underlying meanings; despite Gauguin's advocacy, he could not work easily from his imagination and insisted on the importance of direct experience from nature as his initial inspiration.

64   *Hollyhocks in a One-eared Vase*   1886

sbl. Vincent   91 x 51 cm/35 3/4 x 20 in
Kunsthaus, Zurich
RA 95

65   *Quarry on Montmartre*   1886

ns.   56 x 62 cm/22 x 24 1/2 in
Rijksmuseum Vincent Van Gogh, Amsterdam
RA 94

66   *Outskirts of Paris: Road with Peasant Shouldering a Spade*   1887

ns.   48 x 73 cm/19 x 28 3/4 in
Private Collection

67   *Portrait of Père Tanguy*   1887

ns.   65 x 51 cm/25 1/2 x 20 in
Private Collection
RA 98

68   *The Poet's Garden, Arles*   1888

ns. 73 x 92 cm/28 3/4 x 36 in
Anonymous Lender
RA 100

69   *The Novel Reader*   1888

ns.   73 x 92 cm/28 3/4 x 36 1/4 in
Collection Louis Franck, Chalet Arno, Gstaad,
Switzerland
RA 102

70   *Portrait of Patience Escalier*   1888

ns.   69 x 56 cm/27 1/4 x 22 in
Private Collection

71   *Snowy Landscape with Arles in the
Background*   1888

sbc. Vincent   50 x 60 cm/19 3/4 x 23 1/2 in
Private Collection, England
RA 99

72   *The Tarascon Coaches*   1888

  ns.   72 x 92 cm/28 1/4 x 36 1/4 in
  Henry and Rose Pearlman Foundation, Inc.
  (illustrated in color)

73   *The Wheat Field*   1888

  ns.   73 x 93 cm/28 3/4 x 36 1/2 in
  The Toledo Museum of Art, Ohio
  Gift of Edward Drummond Libbey

74 *Rain* 1889

  ns. 73.5 x 92.5 cm/29 x 36 1/2 in
  Collection Henry P. McIlhenny

75 *Road Menders at Saint Rémy* 1889

  ns. 71 x 93 cm/28 x 36 1/2 in
  The Phillips Collection, Washington
  RA 105

76   *Self-Portrait with Bandaged Ear*   1889

ns.   51 x 45 cm/20 x 17 3/4 in
Private Collection

77   *Still Life, Roses*   1890

ns.   71 x 90 cm/28 x 35 1/2 in
W. Averell Harriman Collection
(illustrated in color)

Charles Angrand 1854–1926

Angrand came from Normandy. After treating rural themes in a style reminiscent of Bastien-Lepage in the early 1880s, he moved through impressionism into a pointillist style in 1886–1887, when he was in close contact with Seurat and Signac, and with van Gogh. He virtually gave up painting in favor of drawing or the use of pastels after 1891. He shared the anarchistic beliefs of many of the neo-impressionists and favored subjects of industrial suburbs or rural peasantry.

78 *The Western Railway at its Exit from Paris (View from the Fortifications)* 1886

La Ligne de l'ouest à sa sortie de Paris (vue prise des fortifications)
sdbr and insc. Paris—86 Ch. Angrand
size on canvas 73 x 92 cm/28 3/4 x 36 1/4 in
Private Collection
RA 5

Gaston La Touche 1854–1913

La Touche's rise to a leading position within French
painting at the end of the nineteenth century was
meteoric. His success depended on his supreme skills
as a colorist and his choice of subject matter.
Exploiting the current fashion for Brittany and for the
eighteenth century, he produced easel paintings,
pastels, and monumental decorative schemes in which
pious Breton peasants succeeded *fêtes galantes* and
pierrots, each treated with a lavish, evocative palette.

79   *Pardon in Brittany*   1896

Pardon en Bretagne
sdbl. G. La Touche 96
100.5 x 110.5 cm/39 1/2 x 43 1/2 in
Art Institute of Chicago, Mr. and Mrs. Martin A.
Ryerson Collection
RA 112

Henri Edmond Cross   1856–1910

Originally from Douai, Cross settled in Paris in 1881
and based his style initially on that of Bastien-Lepage
and then on impressionism. He adopted the pointillist
technique of the neo-impressionists in 1890–1891 and
used it with increasing freedom in later years, creating
rich decorative patterns and color contrasts to express
the light of the Mediterranean coast, where he was
based from 1891. His art had an important influence on
Matisse in 1904.

80   *La Pointe de la Galère*   1891/1892

sbl. Henri Edmond Cross   63.5 x 91.5 cm/25 x 36 in
Private Collection
RA 54

Henry Moret   1856–1913

Moret studied under Laurens in Paris but quickly
discarded his academic training in favor of
impressionism. In 1888 he met Gauguin and Bernard
in Pont-Aven, and by the following summer he had
adopted a modified form of Gauguin's style. By 1894,
however, he had reverted to a robust form of
impressionism, brought about by the absence of his
mentor, Gauguin, since 1891, and perhaps also because
of Moret's adoption by Monet's dealer, Durand-Ruel.
Moret is noted for his renderings of characteristic
Breton subjects such as farmyard scenes and figures
awaiting the return of the fishing fleet.

81   *Waiting for the Fishermen, Brittany*   1894

L'Attente du retour des pêcheurs en Bretagne
sdbl. Henry Moret 94   54 x 65 cm/21 1/4 x 25 1/2 in
Petit Palais, Geneva
RA 149

Maximilien Luce 1858–1941

Originally a wood engraver, Luce learned painting from Carolus-Duran and others, and in 1887 he adopted the pointillist technique, after meeting Seurat, Signac, and the Pissarros. In his later paintings, he reverted to a looser, more impressionistic style. A committed anarchist, he painted many urban and industrial scenes, responding both to their squalor and to their grandeur.

82 *Outskirts of Montmartre* 1887

Environs de Montmartre
sdbr. Luce 87   45.5 x 81 cm/18 x 32 in
Rijksmuseum Kröller-Müller, Otterlo, The Netherlands
RA 117

83 *Coastal Scene* 1893

Bord de mer
sdbr. Luce 93   65 x 92 cm/25 1/2 x 36 1/4 in
Petit Palais, Geneva
RA 118

Georges Seurat   1859–1891

Seurat studied under a pupil of Ingres at the Ecole des Beaux-Arts. He lived all his life in Paris, where he treated modern urban and suburban subjects, in drawings and small studies before 1884 and thereafter in a sequence of major canvases. In the summers between 1885 and 1890 he regularly painted landscapes on the coast. Initially influenced in his paintings by the impressionists, he evolved his pointillist technique in 1885–1886, after meeting Signac. This technique, christened neo-impressionism, was used as a means of systematizing impressionist procedures, in the light of scientific theories on color. In his later figure paintings, Seurat became concerned with the expressive properties of the directions of lines and treated forms in an increasingly stylized, decorative way. His figure paintings convey an ironic sense of the artificiality of urban entertainments, while his landscapes, though carefully composed, remain a more direct response to light and atmosphere.

84   *Sunset*   1881

Coucher de soleil
stamped br. Seurat   oil on panel
15.5 x 25 cm/6 x 9 1/2 in
The City of Bristol Museum and Art Gallery, England
RA 194

85   *Forest of Barbizon*   c. 1883

Forèt de Barbizon
stamped br. Seurat
oil on panel   16 x 25 cm/6 1/4 x 9 1/2 in
Collection Mr. and Mrs. Alexander Lewyt
RA 196

86   *Horses in the River*   1883

Chevaux dans le fleuve
ns. oil on panel   16 x 25 cm/6 1/4 x 9 1/2 in
Private Collection, on loan to the National Gallery, London
RA 197

87   *L'Ile de la Grande Jatte*   1884

sdbl. Seurat 84   65 x 81.5 cm/25 1/2 x 32 in
Collection Mr. and Mrs. John Hay Whitney

88   *Couple Walking*   1884/1885

Couple se promenant
ns.   81 x 65 cm/32 x 25 1/2 in
Anonymous Lender
RA 198

89 *The Lighthouse at Honfleur* 1886

L'Hospice et le phare, Honfleur
sbl. Seurat
65 x 81.5 cm/25 1/2 x 32 in
Collection Mr. and Mrs. Paul Mellon
(illustrated in color)

90 *Port-en-Bessin, the Outer Harbor, Low
Tide* 1888

Port-en-Bessin, l'avant-port, marée basse
sbl. Seurat   53.5 x 65.5 cm/21 x 25 3/4 in
The St. Louis Art Museum

91 *Young Woman Powdering Herself* 1888/1890

Jeune femme se poudrant
sbr. Seurat   94.5 x 79 cm/37 1/4 x 31 in
Courtauld Institute Galleries, London
RA 204

92 *Le Crotoy, Looking Downstream* 1889

Le Crotoy, amont
s on rev. Seurat   70.5 x 86.5 cm/27 3/4 x 34 in, plus
painted frame
Detroit Institute of Arts, Bequest of Robert H.
Tannahill
RA 203

93 *Le Crotoy, Looking Upstream* 1889

Le Crotoy, aval
sbr on border. Seurat   70.5 x 86.5 cm/27 x 34 in
Private Collection
RA 202

94 *The Eiffel Tower* 1889

La Tour Eiffel
ns. oil on panel   24 x 15 cm/9 1/2 x 6 in
The Fine Arts Museums of San Francisco, William H.
Noble Bequest Fund
RA 201

Edmond Aman-Jean   1860–1936

Aman-Jean studied under Lehmann at the Ecole des
Beaux-Arts, Paris, where he met Seurat with whom he
shared a studio for several years. He also worked with
Puvis de Chavannes, assisting him in the execution of
The Sacred Grove (1884, Musée des Beaux-Arts, Lyon).
Apart from exhibiting regularly at the Paris Salons,
Aman-Jean also belonged to the symbolist circle of
artists and writers around Mallarmé. This association
may have affected the way in which Aman-Jean
resolved the problem of a balance between the real
and the ideal in painting; in the 1890s he relied upon
the suggestion of mood and an emphasis on
decoration rather than upon a literal description of his
subjects. After c. 1912, his work was increasingly
influenced by Bonnard.

95   *Portrait de Mlle. Thadée C. Jacquet*   1892

sbl. Aman-Jean   112.5 x 89.5 cm/44 1/4 x 35 1/4 in
Musée d'Orsay, Paris
RA 3

Louis Anquetin   1861–1932

Born in Normandy, Anquetin moved to Paris in c.
1882, studying first under Bonnat and then at the
Atelier Cormon where he met Toulouse-Lautrec,
Bernard, and van Gogh. He established a reputation as
a brilliant, innovative artist, the friend of leading
symbolist writers and the leader of a café-cabaret
circle centered on Aristide Bruant's Le Mirliton in
Montmartre. Initially an impressionist, Anquetin
joined with Bernard in the winter of 1886–1887 to
reject all naturalistic styles of painting and evolved
cloisonnism, the precursor of pictorial symbolism, by
summer 1887. His subjects included townscapes, café
scenes, nudes, the racecourse, and fashionable
women. He later absorbed and discarded in quick
succession styles derived from Lautrec and Renoir,
and by c. 1896 Anquetin finally settled on a baroque
style of painting derived from Peter Paul Rubens.

96   *Street—Five O'Clock in the Evening*   1887
Rue—cinq heures du soir
sdbl. L. Anquetin 1887   69 x 53.5 cm/27 1/4 x 21 in
Wadsworth Atheneum, Hartford, Connecticut,
Ella Gallup Sumner and Mary Catlin Sumner
Collection
RA 7   *(illustrated in color)*

Jacques Emile Blanche   1861–1942

Son of a noted pathologist, Blanche always lived in Paris, but regularly visited Dieppe. He gained great success as a fashionable portraitist, working in a free painterly style much influenced by Manet and comparable to the technique of John Singer Sargent. His contacts with Britain, and his hospitality at Dieppe, made him a focus for Anglo-French artistic relations, described in his volumes of autobiography.

97   *Head of a Young Girl*   1885

Tête de jeune fille
sbdr and insc. J. E. Blanche 1885 To my friend Sickert
55 x 45 cm/21 1/2 x 17 3/4 in
Private Collection, Wales
RA 24

98   *Portrait of Aubrey Beardsley*   1895

Portrait d'Aubrey Beardsley
sdbr and insc. J. E. Blanche Dieppe 95
90 x 72 cm/35 1/2 x 28 3/4 in
National Portrait Gallery, London
RA 25

Aristide Maillol 1861–1944

Maillol had always intended to be a painter. He
trained in Perpignan and then attended the Ecole des
Beaux-Arts in Paris. Swept up in the debate over style
in the 1880s, Maillol moved from landscapes executed
in somber, Barbizon tones to an admiration for
impressionism and the work of Puvis de Chavannes.
By 1889, friendship with Daniel de Monfreid brought
him into contact with Gauguin, and in 1892 he became
a member of the nabis, adopting their flat, decorative
style. Failing eyesight in the later 1890s caused him to
turn to sculpture; he won great fame after 1900 for his
monumental classicizing figures.

99   *The Crown of Flowers*   1892/1893

La Couronne de fleurs
ns.   130 x 161 cm/51 1/4 x 63 1/2 in
Josefowitz Collection, Switzerland

Lucien Simon   1861–1945

Born in Paris, Simon was known both for his Breton
subjects and for his paintings of fashionable Parisian
genre scenes. Simon visited Brittany for the first time
in 1890 after marrying the sister of the Breton painter
André Dauchez. In 1895, his admiration for the work
of Charles Cottet led him to introduce himself to this
artist, and together with Dauchez and others, they
came to form the "black school of painting," or "La
Bande noire." Using their typical dark palette, Simon
sought in his paintings of Brittany to capture the harsh
existence, imbued with deep piety, characteristic of
that backward region of France.

100   *The Procession*   1901

La Procession
sbl. L. Simon   136 x 175 cm/53 1/2 x 69 in
Musée d'Orsay, Paris
RA 217

Paul Ranson 1862–1909

Cofounder of the nabis, Ranson entered the Ecole des Arts Décoratifs in 1886 and then attended the Académie Julian. In his studio, the nabis held their group meetings, at which philosophy, religion, Theosophy, and art in general were discussed extensively. Like that of the other nabis, Ranson's artistic output included easel and decorative paintings, tapestries, ceramics, book illustrations, as well as stage sets and costumes for puppet theaters. One year before his death he founded the Académie Ranson, where Denis, Bonnard, Sérusier, Félix Vallotton, Maillol, and Théo van Rysselberghe taught.

101 *Christ and Buddha* c. 1890

Christ et Boudha
ns: insc in Arabic bcr. *furusiya nabiy* [knighthood of prophets]
72.5 x 51.5 cm/28 1/2 x 20 1/4 in
Collection Arthur G. Altschul
RA 163

Charles Cottet 1863–1924

Born in Le Puy, Cottet trained under Puvis de
Chavannes and Alfred Philippe Roll in Paris. He
exhibited for the first time at the Salon of 1889.
However, it was at the Salon of 1893 that his
distinctive treatment of Breton subjects was noted.
Cottet visited Brittany regularly after 1885, and his
paintings capture the grandeur and melancholy of its
landscapes, the harshness of existence, and the major
events of peasant life. His masterly use of a dark,
emotive palette during the 1890s established him as
the leader of a group of artists, including Simon and
Dauchez, known as "La Bande noire."

102   *Evening Light: the Port of Camaret*   1892

Rayons du soir: port de Camaret
sdbr. Ch. Cottet [? . . .] 1892
72 x 110 cm/28 1/4 x 43 1/4 in
Musée du Louvre, Paris
RA 51

103   *The People of Ouessant Watching Over a Dead
Child*   1899

Gens d'Ouessant veillant un enfant mort
sbr. Ch. Cottet   91 x 125 cm/35 3/4 x 49 in
Musée du Petit Palais, Paris
RA 53

Lucien Pissarro 1863–1944

Eldest son of Camille Pissarro, Lucien adopted
Seurat's neo-impressionist technique, along with his
father, in 1886. In 1890, he moved to London, where he
mixed with the Arts and Crafts circle and founded the
Eragny Press in 1894. His technique became looser and
more impressionistic after 1890. He became an
important influence on young English painters after c.
1906, serving as an intermediary between them and
French impressionism.

104 *The Rue Saint-Vincent, Winter Sunshine* 1890

La Rue Saint-Vincent, soleil d'hiver
sdbr. Lucien Pissarro 1890
65.5 x 81.5 cm/25 3/4 x 32 in
Flint Institute of Arts, Michigan, Gift of the Whiting
Foundation
RA 158

Paul Signac   1863–1935

Signac lived in the Paris area until 1892, when he
moved his base to Saint-Tropez on the Mediterranean.
Influenced in his early paintings by impressionism, he
met Seurat in 1884 and adopted the neo-impressionist
technique in 1885–1886, painting initially in small
points of clear color. His technique broadened greatly
after c. 1892, and he came to emphasize bold contrasts
of intense color in his southern scenes. He worked
with van Gogh around Paris in 1887 and with Matisse
at Saint-Tropez in 1904. He was a convinced anarchist
and an important figure in the organization of the
jury-free exhibitions of the Indépendants. His book
D'Eugène Delacroix au néo-impressionnisme of 1899
is the most important theoretical justification of
neo-impressionism.

105   *The Railway Junction at Bois-Colombes*   1886

L'Embranchement à Bois-Colombes
sdbr. P. Signac 86; insc bl. Op 130 R. Darzens
33 x 47 cm/13 x 18 in
Leeds City Art Galleries, England
RA 206

106   *The Dining Room*   1886/1887

La Salle à manger
sdbl. 86 P. Signac 87; insc br. Op. 152
89 x 115 cm/35 x 45 1/4 in
Rijksmuseum Kröller-Müller, Otterlo, The Netherlands
RA 208

107   *The Bridge at Asnières*
(The Stern of The Tub in the Sun)   1888

Le Pont d'Asnières (L'arrière du Tub, soleil)
sdbl. P. Signac 88; insc br. Op. 175
46 x 65 cm/18 x 25 1/2 in
Collection Sir Jack Lyons, CBE
RA 209

108   *Against the Enamel of a Background Rhythmic*
      with Beats and Angles, Tones and Colors,
      Portrait of M. Félix Fénéon in 1890   1890

      Sur l'email d'un fond rhythmique de mesures et
      d'angles, de tons et de teintes, portrait de M. Félix
      Fénéon en 1890
      sdbr. P. Signac 90; insc bl. Op. 217
      73.5 x 92.5 cm/29 x 36 1/2 in
      Private Collection, New York
      RA 211

109   *Presto (finale) or Breeze, Concarneau*   1891

      Presto (finale) or Brise, Concarneau
      sdbl. P. Signac 91; insc br. Op. 222
      66.5 x 82 cm/26 1/4 x 32 1/4 in
      The Estate of Sir Charles Clore
      RA 212 *(illustrated in color)*

110   *Saint-Tropez*   1893

      sbl. P. Signac; insc on rev. P.S. St Tropez   oil and
      pencil on panel
      19 x 27 cm/7 1/2 x 10 1/2 in
      Courtauld Institute Galleries, London
      RA 213

111 *Poppies* c. 1894

Les Coquelicots
ns. oil on panel 15 x 24 cm/6 x 9 1/2 in
Private Collection, Paris
RA 214

112 *Saint-Tropez, Pine Wood* 1896

Saint-Tropez, bois de pins
sdbl. P. Signac 96 65 x 81 cm/25 1/2 x 32 in
Musée de l'Annonciade, Saint-Tropez, France
RA 215

Lucien Lévy-Dhurmer   1864–1953

After a successful early career as a lithographer and decorator, Lévy-Dhurmer was inspired by classical art while visiting Italy in 1895 and decided to become a painter. His one-man show at the Galerie Georges Petit in Paris in 1896 established him as a gifted pastelist, a fashionable portraitist capable of extreme verisimilitude, and a painter of subjects drawn from mythology or inspired by Ludwig van Beethoven, Claude Debussy, and Gabriel Fauré.

113   *Our Lady of Penmarc'h*   1896

Notre-Dame de Penmarc'h
sdbr. L. Levy-Dhurmer 1896
41 x 33 cm/16 1/4 x 13 in
The picture is shown in its original dark wood frame, decorated with a rustic Breton geometric design and the engraved inscription "Notre-Dame de Penmarc'h."
Collection M. Michel Perinet, Paris
RA 116

Paul Sérusier 1864–1927

Sérusier received a traditional training at the
Académie Julian and exhibited a conventional
painting at the Salon of 1888. Later that year he met
Gauguin in Brittany, an encounter which produced the
radically simplified, nonnaturalistic interpretation of
the landscape outside Pont-Aven, *The Talisman,*
which became the manifesto for Sérusier and his
friends at the Académie Julian—Denis, Ranson,
Bonnard, and Henri Ibels. Together they formed the
nabis, or prophets, and were joined in 1889 by Vuillard
and Ker-Xavier Roussel. Sérusier's intelligence and
friendship with Gauguin established him as a leader of
this group. He frequently painted in Brittany in the
1890s; however his close analysis of styles of
nonnaturalistic painting led him to absorb lessons
from Puvis de Chavannes and Cézanne as well as
Gauguin. By 1900 he had adopted the sacred systems
of proportion and color relationships elaborated by the
School of Beuron and expounded in his own book
ABC de la peinture (1921).

114   *The Breton Weaver*   1888

Le Tisserand breton
sdbl. Sérusier 1888   72 x 59 cm/28 1/4 x 23 1/4 in
Musée du Haubergier, Senlis, France
RA 186

115   *The Talisman*   1888

Le Talisman
insc on rev. Fait en Octobre 1888 sous la Direction de
Paul Gauguin par P. Sérusier Pont-Aven [Executed in
October 1888 under the guidance of Paul Gauguin by
P. Sérusier Pont-Aven]
oil on panel   27 x 22 cm/10 3/4 x 8 3/4 in
Collection J. F. Denis, France
RA 187

116 *Pont-Aven Triptych* 1892/1893

Triptych Pont-Aven
ns. 33 x 73 cm/28 3/4 x 52 1/4 in overall
Collection Jean Claude Bellier
RA 191

117 *Young Bretons in the Bois d'Amour* 1893

Le Bébé et les grandes soeurs
sbl. P. Sérusier
71 x 91.5 cm/28 x 36 in
Josefowitz Collection, Switzerland

Henri de Toulouse-Lautrec   1864–1901

As famous for his lithographs as for his paintings, Toulouse-Lautrec came from an aristocratic family near Albi and trained under René Princeteau, Bonnat, and Fernand Cormon, in whose studio he met Anquetin, Bernard, and van Gogh. By 1884, Montmartre had become the focus of his life. He acquired a studio there and became a member of Anquetin's café-cabaret circle centered on Aristide Bruant's café, Le Mirliton, and from then on local scenes of prostitution and popular entertainment became his prime subject matter. Neither satirical nor critical, Toulouse-Lautrec's vision of these subcultures of Paris expressed sympathy and understanding, conveyed in compositions which combine witty draftsmanship with asymmetrical groupings reminiscent of Degas. This attitude is also evident in his many portraits, almost all of which depict his friends. Two riding accidents as a child stunted his growth, and later in life he became an alcoholic.

118   *Ball at the Moulin Rouge*   1890

Bal au Moulin Rouge
sdtr. HTLautrec 90   115.5 x 150 cm/45 1/2 x 59 in
Collection Henry P. McIlhenny

(illustrated in color)

119   *Quadrille at the Moulin Rouge*   1892

Quadrille au Moulin Rouge
sbr. HTL (in monogram)
gouache on cardboard
80 x 60.5 cm/31 1/2 x 23 3/4 in
National Gallery of Art, Washington, Chester Dale Collection

120   *Rue des Moulins*   1894

sbr. HTL (in monogram)
oil on cardboard mounted on wood
83.5 x 61.5 cm/33 x 24 in
National Gallery of Art, Washington, Chester Dale
Collection

121   *Messaline Seated*   1901

Messaline assise
stamped bl. HTL   96 x 77.5 cm/38 1/2 x 31 in
Henry and Rose Pearlman Foundation, Inc.
RA 225

Félix Vallotton   1865–1925

Although Vallotton was Swiss by birth, the most
significant years of his life were spent in Paris, where
he arrived in 1882 to study at the Ecole des Beaux-Arts
and the Académie Julian. Influenced by Charles
Maurin and the 1890 exhibition of Japanese art at the
Ecole des Beaux-Arts, Vallotton discarded his somber,
meticulously realistic painting style of c. 1891 in favor
of radically simplified woodcuts and lithographs. He
transferred to his paintings of the 1890s the style, and
frequently also the subject matter, of these prints.
Apart from exhibiting at the first Salon de la Rose +
Croix, Vallotton also became a nabi and participated in
the group's exhibitions. By c. 1901 he virtually ceased
to produce prints, devoting himself to paintings of
classical nudes and large, carefully composed
landscapes.

122   *Félix Fénéon in the Offices of the "Revue
blanche"*   1896

Félix Fénéon au bureau de la "Revue blanche"
sdtl. F. Vallotton 96   oil on board
52.5 x 66 cm/20 3/4 x 26 in
Josefowitz Collection, Switzerland
RA 273

123   *Intimacy: Interior with Lovers and a
Screen*   1898

Intimité: Intérieur avec amants et paravent
sdblc. F. Vallotton 98   oil on board
35 x 57 cm/13 3/4 x 22 1/2 in
Josefowitz Collection, Switzerland
RA 274

Pierre Bonnard 1867–1947

Bonnard attended the Ecole des Beaux-Arts and the Académie Julian, where he met Sérusier, Denis, Ranson, and Ibels. His early work is naturalistic in treatment, but by c. 1890 he had evolved an individual style of nonnaturalistic painting based on careful study of Sérusier's *The Talisman*, Gauguin's recent work at the Café Volpini exhibition (1889), Japanese art, and a skittish sense of fun. A founding member of the nabis, Bonnard shared Vuillard's interest in the interpretation of everyday events to reveal underlying emotions, as well as the group's general commitment to the applied arts. Like Vuillard, he responded to the disintegration of the nabis in c. 1900 by a return to greater naturalism. After c. 1910 he evolved a style distinguished by the lavish use of color.

124   *Bouquet of Wild Flowers*   c. 1888

     Bouquet des champs
     sbl. P. Bonnard   38 x 33 cm/15 3/4 x 13 in
     Private Collection
     RA 27

125   *House with a Turret (Château de Vizien)*   1888

     Maison à la tourelle (Château de Vizien)
     sbl. Pierre Bonnard   19 x 29 cm/7 1/2 x 11 1/2 in
     Private Collection
     RA 26

126   *Paris, Rue de Parme on Bastille Day, 1890*   1890
ns.   79.5 x 40 cm/31 1/4 x 15 3/4 in
Collection Mr. and Mrs. Paul Mellon

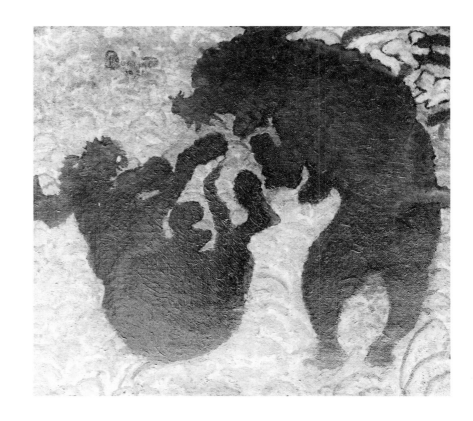

127 *Woman in a Cape*   c. 1891

Femme à la pèlerine
stl. PB oil on paper glued to canvas
160 x 48 cm/63 x 19 in
Mrs. Florence Gould, U.S.A.
RA 31

128 *Woman in a Check Dress*   c. 1891

Femme à la robe quadrillée
stl. PB oil on paper glued on canvas
160 x 48 cm/63 x 19 in
Mrs. Florence Gould, U.S.A.
RA 30

129 *Two Dogs Playing*   1891

Deux chiens jouant
sdcl. P. Bonnard 1891   37 x 39.5 cm/14 1/2 x 15 1/2 in
Southampton Art Gallery, England
RA 29

130   *The Barrel Organ Grinder*   1895

Le Joueur d'organe
sdbc. 95 P. Bonnard   oil on panel
41 x 26 cm/16 x 10 1/4 in
Anonymous Lender
RA 32

131   *The Red Garters*   c. 1904

Les Jarretières rouges
sbl. Bonnard   61 x 50 cm/24 x 19 1/2 in
Private Collection, Switzerland
RA 34

Ker-Xavier Roussel   1867–1944

A student at the Lycée Condorcet with Vuillard, Denis, and Lugné-Poë, Roussel trained at the Ecole des Beaux-Arts and then at the Académie Julian, where he became a member of the nabis in 1889. Reticent by nature, Roussel did not participate as actively as the other nabis in their group activities, although he shared their interest in decorative painting and in making original prints. In the early 1890s, his technique and focus on intimate, domestic scenes owed much to Vuillard, although he was also impressed by the flat blocks of color found in Vallotton's paintings. By 1900, like Denis, he reacted to the disintegration of the nabis by returning to more classical themes, often executed on a large scale.

132   *The Seamstresses' Workshop*   c. 1894

L'Atelier de couture
sbr. K. X. Roussel   112 x 76.5 cm/44 x 20 in
Collection Arthur G. Altschul
RA 182

Emile Bernard   1868–1941

After attending the Ecole des Arts Décoratifs, Bernard
joined the Atelier Cormon in 1884 where he met
Toulouse-Lautrec, Anquetin, and van Gogh. Expelled
for insubordinate behavior in spring 1886, he traveled
through Normandy and Brittany, meeting
Schuffenecker at Concarneau and Gauguin at
Pont-Aven. He passed swiftly through impressionism
and neo-impressionism, evolving cloisonnism with
Anquetin in the summer of 1887, followed by a form of
pictorial symbolism in 1888 that helped Gauguin
create his *Vision After the Sermon*. Between 1888 and
1891, Bernard and Gauguin worked closely together,
both exhibiting at the Café Volpini in 1889. After a
brief association with the nabis during 1891-1893, and
inclusion in the first Salon de la Rose + Croix in 1892,
Bernard went to Egypt in 1893. By 1900 he had
adopted a traditional style indebted to Titian.

133   *The Iron Bridges*   1887

Les Ponts de fer
sdbr. E. Bernard 1887   46 x 54 cm/18 x 21 3/4 in
The Museum of Modern Art, New York,
Grace Rainey Rogers Fund, 1962
RA 12

134   *Portrait of Père Tanguy*   1887

Portrait du Père Tanguy
sdtl. Emile Bernard 1887; insc tr. à mon ami Tanguy
36 x 31 cm/14 1/4 x 12 1/4 in
Kunstmuseum, Basel, Switzerland
RA 13

135   *Breton Women at a Pardon*   1888

Bretonnes au pardon
sdbl. E. Bernard 1888   74 x 92 cm/29 x 36 1/4 in
Private Collection, Paris
RA 15

136   *The Buckwheat Harvest*   1888

Le Blé noir
sdbrc. Emile Bernard 1888
72 x 92 cm/28 1/4 x 35 1/2 in
Josefowitz Collection, Switzerland
RA 17

137   *Self-Portrait, for his Friend Vincent*   1888

Autoportrait, à son copaing Vincent
sd and insc tr. Emile Bernard 1888 à son copaing
Vincent
46 x 55 cm/18 x 21 3/4 in
Rijksmuseum Vincent Van Gogh, Amsterdam
RA 16

138   *Bathers*   1890

Baigneuses
sdbr. Emile Bernard 90
32 x 41.5 cm/12 3/4 x 16 1/4 in
Private Collection, London
RA 18

139   *Harvest by the Sea*   1891

Moisson au bord de la mer
sbr. E. Bernard; dbc. 1891
54 x 73 cm/21 1/4 x 28 3/4 in
Collection Mr. and Mrs. Robert Walker
RA 19

140   *Breton Women on a Wall*   1892

Bretonnes sur un mur
sdbl. Emile Bernard 1892   83 x 115 cm/32 1/2 x 45 in
Josefowitz Collection, Switzerland
RA 20

Georges Lacombe 1868–1916

Lacombe was born at Versailles into comfortable and cultivated circumstances. Although he trained at the Académie Julian he only met Sérusier in 1892, an event which led to his adoption as a member of the nabis ("le nabi sculpteur"). He worked regularly in Brittany between 1888 and 1897, painting in a style influenced by Japanese art, and evolved an archaizing style of woodcarving inspired in part by Gauguin's polychrome sculpture.

141   *Blue Seascape—Effect of Waves*   c. 1894

Marine bleue, effet de vagues
sbr. GL   tempera on canvas
49 x 65 cm/19 1/4 x 25 1/2 in
Musée des Beaux-Arts de Rennes, France
RA 111

Edouard Vuillard   1868–1940

Educated at the Lycée Cordorcet, where he met Denis,
Roussel, and Lugné-Poë, Vuillard enrolled at the Ecole
des Beaux-Arts in 1887. Entering the Académie Julian
after the formation of the nabis, Vuillard was quickly
absorbed into the group; he participated in their
exhibitions at Le Barc de Boutteville's gallery and
Bing's Maison de l'Art Nouveau, and he shared their
enthusiasm for the decorative arts. Friendship with
Lugné-Poë, the actor and impresario, brought
commissions for stage sets, costumes, and theater
programs for the symbolist Théâtre de l'Oeuvre. His
subjects, like Bonnard's, were intimate. Vuillard favored
quiet interiors in which domestic routine was expressed
by overall patterns of color that become the symbolic
manifestation of underlying emotions and psychological
states. Also like Bonnard, Vuillard turned toward greater
naturalism after the disintegration of the nabis in
c. 1900.

142   *The Reader*   c. 1890

Le Liseur
ns; atelier stamp bl. L2497a   oil on board
35 x 19 cm/13 3/4 x 7 1/2 in
Private Collection, Paris
RA 230

143   *Self-Portrait*   c. 1890

Autoportrait
ns; atelier stamp br. L2497a   oil on octagonal
cardboard
36 x 28 cm/14 1/4 x 11 in
Private Collection, Paris
RA 229

144 *The Stevedores* c. 1890

Les Débardeurs
sbr. E. Vuillard   45 x 61 cm/17 3/4 x 24 in
Collection Arthur G. Altschul
RA 231

145 *Little Girls Walking* c. 1891

Filles se promenant
sblc. E. Vuillard   81 x 65 cm/32 x 25 1/2 in
Private Collection, Switzerland
RA 233 *(illustrated in color)*

146   *The Outspoken Dinner Party (After the Meal)*   c. 1891

Le Dîner vert (Après le repas)
sbr. E. Vuillard   34 x 49 cm/13 1/2 x 19 1/4 in
Private Collection
RA 235

148   *Portrait of Lugné-Poë*   1891

Portrait de Lugné-Poë
sdbl. EV 91   oil on paper mounted on panel
22 x 26.5 cm/8 3/4 x 10 1/2 in
Memorial Art Gallery of the University of Rochester,
New York, Gift of Fletcher Steele
RA 234

147   *The Landing, rue de Miromesnil*   1891

Le Palier, rue de Miromesnil
sdtr. e. vuillard 91   40.5 x 23 cm/16 x 9 in
Collection Mrs. Samuel Godfrey
RA 232

149   *Mother and Sister of the Artist*   c. 1892

Mère et soeur de l'artiste
sbr. E. Vuillard   46.5 x 56.5 cm/18 1/4 x 22 1/4 in
The Museum of Modern Art, New York, Gift of Mrs.
Sadie A. May 1934
RA 236

150   *Madame Vuillard Sewing*   1895

Madame Vuillard cousant
sdbc. E. Vuillard '95   oil on board
32 x 36 cm/12 1/2 x 14 1/4 in
Private Collection, England
RA 237

151   *Seated Woman*   c. 1901

Femme assise
sbr. E. Vuillard   oil on board mounted on panel
77.5 x 51 cm/30 1/2 x 20 in
Private Collection
RA 238

152   *The Painter Ker-Xavier Roussel and his Daughter*   c. 1904

Le Peintre Ker-Xavier Roussel et sa fille
sbr. E. Vuillard   oil on cardboard
57 x 52 cm/23 x 21 in
Albright-Knox Art Gallery, Buffalo, New York,
Room of Contemporary Art Fund, 1959

Henri Matisse   1869–1954

After training as a lawyer, Matisse took up painting in 1890 and studied under Moreau at the Ecole des Beaux-Arts. After 1897, he began to use brighter colors and more varied brushwork, under the influence of impressionism and neo-impressionism. Then, following an interlude of more somber painting in 1901–1903, he adopted a dazzling, nonnaturalistic palette in 1904–1905 on successive visits to the Mediterranean, while working with Signac and Cross in 1904, and particularly while staying with André Derain at Collioure in 1905. These exchanges led to the birth of fauvism. Throughout his career Matisse insisted on the primacy of decorative qualities in painting, suggesting space by rich harmonies of pattern and color. He evolved his later styles through the study of Cézanne and Moslem art as well as through many other stimuli.

153   *Woman Looking After a Pig*   1896

Femme gardant un cochon
sdbr. H. Matisse 1896   59.5 x 73 cm/23 1/2 x 28 3/4 in
Musée Matisse, Cimiez, Nice, France
RA 128

154   *First Orange Still Life*   1898/1899

Première nature morte orange
sbr. H. Matisse   56 x 73 cm/22 x 28 3/4 in
Musée National d'Art Moderne — Centre Georges Pompidou, Paris
RA 130

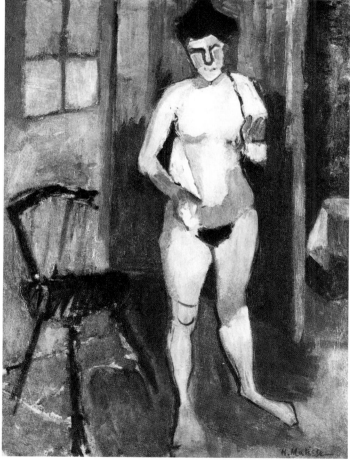

155 *Standing Nude* 1901

Nu debout
sbr. H. Matisse 81 x 59.5 cm/32 x 23 1/2 in
Collection Mr. and Mrs. Gifford Phillips

156 *Open Window, Collioure* 1905

Fenêtre ouverte à Collioure
sbr. Henri-Matisse 55.5 x 46 cm/21 3/4 x 18 in
Collection Mr. and Mrs. John Hay Whitney

157 *Young Sailor I* 1906

Le Jeune marin I
sbl. Henri Matisse 100 x 78.5 cm/39 1/4 x 32 3/4 in
Private Collection
RA 132 *(illustrated in color)*

158 *Young Sailor II* 1906

Le Jeune marin II
sdbl. Henri Mattise 1906
100 x 81 cm/39 1/2 x 32 in
Collection Mr. and Mrs. Jacques Gelman, Mexico City
(illustrated in color)

Maurice Denis   1870–1943

Educated at the Lycée Condorcet where he met
Vuillard, Roussel, and Lugné-Poë, Denis studied at the
Atelier Balla and then at the Académie Julian. There
he met Sérusier, Ranson, Bonnard, and Ibels, with
whom he formed the nabis in 1888. Like his fellow
nabis, Denis organized and participated in group
exhibitions, executed both easel and large-scale
decorative paintings, and produced book illustrations,
prints, stained glass designs, stage sets, and costumes.
He propagated the nabis' artistic program in articles
(e.g., "Définition du néo-traditionnisme," 1890) and in
books. In the early 1890s, he shared the flat, patterned
style of the other artists in the group, but later his
work became increasingly influenced by Italian early
Renaissance painting. His art consistently reflects his
Roman Catholicism, and his writings proclaim his
concern for the reform of religious art.

159   *Catholic Mystery*   1890

    Mystère Catholique
    sbl.   Maurice Denis; insc in Greek
    tr. ΑΣΠΑΣΜΟΣ [Hail]
    51 x 77 cm/20 x 30 1/4 in
    Collection J. F. Denis, France
    RA 65

160   *Sunlight on the Terrace*   1890

    Taches de soleil sur la terrasse
    ns; dbr. Oct. 90   oil on board
    20 x 20 cm/7 3/4 x 7 3/4 in
    Private Collection, St. Germain-en-Laye
    RA 66

161   *The Cup of Tea* or *Mystical Allegory*   1892

La Tasse de thé ou *Allégorie mystique*
sdtl. MAUD 92   46 x 55 cm/18 x 21 1/2 in
Private Collection, France
RA 68

162   *Procession Under the Trees*   1892

Procession sous les arbres
sdbr. MAUD 92   56 x 81.5 cm/22 x 32 in
Collection Arthur G. Altschul
RA 67

163   *The Blessing of the Boats*   c. 1895

Baptême des bateaux
sbcr. MAUD   75 x 80 cm/29 1/2 x 31 1/2 in
Josefowitz Collection, Switzerland
RA 70

164   *Bathers*   1899

Baigneuses
sdbl. MAUD 99   73 x 100 cm/28 3/4 x 39 1/2 in
Musée du Petit Palais, Paris
RA 71

Maurice de Vlaminck   1876–1958

A novelist and racing cyclist before he became a
painter, Vlaminck turned to art under the inspiration
of a van Gogh exhibition in 1901. He was self-taught
and evolved a bold painting style, using strong
nonnaturalistic color, when working with Derain in
1904–1905. He adopted clear primary colors after
seeing Matisse and Derain's fauve paintings of
summer 1905, but from c. 1907 on, under the influence
of Cézanne, he turned to more subdued tones, as seen
in the somber, expressive landscapes of his later years.

165   *The Kitchen (Interior)*   1904/1905

> *La Cuisine (intérieur)*
> sbl. Vlaminck   65 x 54 cm/25 1/2 x 21 1/4 in
> Musée National d'Art Moderne — Centre Georges
> Pompidou, Paris
> RA 228

166   *Le Pont de Bezons*   1906

> sbl. Vlaminck
> 67 x 79 cm/26 1/2 x 31 in
> Anonymous Lender

167   *Fishermen at Collioure*   1905

Pêcheurs à Collioure
sbr. A. Derain   46 x 54 cm/18 x 21 1/2 in
Anonymous Lender
RA 73

168   *The River Seine at Chatou*   1905

La Seine à Chatou
sbr. A. Derain   70.5 x 110.5 cm/27 3/4 x 43 in
Kimbell Art Museum, Fort Worth, Texas

André Derain   1880–1954

Born at Chatou near Paris, Derain met Matisse in 1899 and Vlaminck in 1901 after a minor railroad accident. Working with Vlaminck at Chatou in 1904–1905, he evolved a style which used bold brushwork and nonnaturalistic color to express the rhythm and effect of a scene. He spent summer 1905 at Collioure with Matisse, where both men used extremely strong and exaggerated colors to suggest the Mediterranean light; this style was christened fauvism. Influenced subsequently by Gauguin, by Cézanne, and by primitive art, Derain turned to more eclectic and, later, more traditional styles.

169   *The Dance*   c. 1906

La Danse
ns.   185 x 228.5 cm/72 1/2 x 90 in
Private Collection
RA 74

170 *London Bridge*   1906

Pont de Londres
sbl. Derain
65.5 x 98.5 cm/25 3/4 x 38 3/4 in
Private Collection

Pablo Picasso   1881–1973

Trained as a painter in Barcelona, Picasso visited Paris several times after 1900, settling there in 1904. In 1900–1901 he was attracted by the night life of Montmartre, but he turned in 1902–1904 to a sequence of canvases painted in a dominant blue tonality, which expressed the melancholy of the outcasts who formed their subjects. Lighter in tone and less elongated in drawing are his circus paintings of 1904–1905, which gave way in 1906 to works in a dominant pink tonality, representing subjects of a neoclassical order and idealization. In 1907, his *Demoiselles d'Avignon* started him on the path which led him and Georges Braque to cubism.

171   *Woman with Bangs*   1902

Figure de femme aux cheveux frangés
stl. Picasso
59.5 x 49 cm/23 1/2 x 19 1/4 in
The Baltimore Museum of Art, Cone Collection

172   *Nude with Clasped Hands*   1906

Nu aux mains serrées
sd and insc on rev. A mon vrai ami Picasso 1 er Janvier 1907
gouache on canvas   96.5 x 75.5 cm/38 x 29 3/4 in
Art Gallery of Ontario, Toronto, Gift of Sam and Ayala Zacks, 1970
RA 151

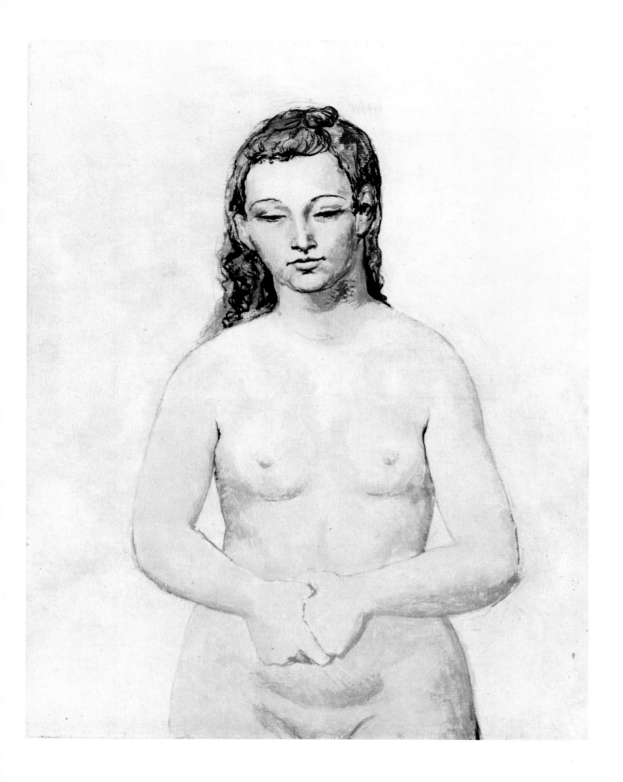

Georges Braque   1882–1963

Brought up in Le Havre, Braque was based in Paris
from 1902, painting first in a style indebted to
impressionism and then, in 1905–1906, coming
under the influence of the fauves, and particularly of
Derain. His freely treated, highly colored paintings of
late 1906 are also a response to the work of Gauguin.
In 1907, the impact of Cézanne's style led him
gradually to use a more muted palette and to focus on
formal structure, a concentration which led him to his
form of cubism by 1908–1909, when he began to work
closely with Picasso.

173   *The Port*   1906

Le Port
sdbl. G. Braque 06   46 x 55 cm/18 x 21 1/2 in
Private Collection
RA 35

33 Redon *The Red Sphinx*

138

77 van Gogh   *Still Life, Roses*

8 Degas   *Portrait of Mademoiselle Hélène Rouart*

145 Vuillard *Little Girls Walking*

52 Gauguin *The Man with the Axe*

118 Toulouse-Lautrec *The Ball at the Moulin Rouge*

96 Anquetin *Street—Five O'Clock in the Evening*

157 Matisse *Young Sailor I*

158 Matisse *Young Sailor II*

23 Monet *Varengeville Church*

5 C. Pissarro *Women Haymaking*

205 Sickert *L'Hôtel Royal, Dieppe*

206 Steer *Boulogne Sands*

224 Pellizza *The Fourth Estate*

216 Morbelli *For Eighty Cents*

109 Signac *Presto (finale)*
or *Breeze, Concarneau*

236 Toorop *The Shell Gatherer*

271 Hassam *Room of Flowers*

257 Homer   *Sleigh Ride*

Germany, Norway, and Switzerland

GILLIAN PERRY

In Germany reactions to French post-impressionism were complex and often subject to regional variations. Writing over twenty years later, Julius Meier-Graefe described "the confused state of mind" of the German artists in 1890:

It is impossible to conceive how riddled with holes our mental communication system was. Toulouse-Lautrec, Vallotton, Odilon Redon, Axel Gallen, Vigeland, Beardsley, Gauguin and Munch, Puvis de Chavannes and Whistler were our main sources of awareness apart from the German romantics.

Access to these "sources of awareness" varied from one provincial center to another. Unlike England or France, where the capital city was also the artistic capital, in Germany the political unification of 1870–1871 was reflected in a cultural decentralization. In the late 1890s Berlin began to emerge as the focus of so-called German impressionism, attracting artists such as Max Liebermann, Fritz von Uhde, Lovis Corinth, and Max Slevogt. At the same time Munich was gaining a reputation as a center for Jugendstil design and symbolist painting, represented in the work of Munich-based artists such as Thomas Theodor Heine and Franz von Stuck.

During the same period many of the larger provincial towns spawned artists' communities in the neighboring countryside. Perhaps the best known of these was Worpswede, established in 1889 in a village north of Bremen. Artists from this group included Otto Modersohn, renowned in the 1890s for his sentimental landscape style known as "nature lyricism" (Naturlyrismus), and his wife Paula Modersohn-Becker. Her works from c. 1902–1907 combine the influence of French post-impressionism, absorbed during trips to Paris, with an iconography rooted in the concerns of the Worpswede colony.

The sudden emergence of regional artists' colonies was related to broader sociocultural developments in Germany at the turn of the century. Reactions against nineteenth-century urban and industrial expansion often took the form of revivals of mysticism and nature cults. These attitudes were nurtured and encouraged by cultural critics such as Julius Langbehn. His Rembrandt as Educator of 1890 was a reactionary but immensely popular book which identified art, and more specifically the artist (for whom Rembrandt stood as a potent symbol), as a regenerative hope in a decadent materialistic society. He believed the artist had a vital role to play by identifying and painting the "natural" unsophisticated forces (which included the indigenous peasant community) in Germany. In addition to providing a raison d'être for rural

174 Liebermann *Eva*

153

artists' colonies, these ideas also permeated the iconography and attitudes of many important figures in the German art world at the time. Corinth's writings, for example, are saturated with Langbehnian ideas, and his tendency to exalt the artist's role was reflected in his repetition of confident self-portraits. A similar tendency can be found in the self-image of the Brücke group, who saw themselves in 1906 as a "new generation of creators."

Most of the regional artists' groups were formed in a loose spirit of antiacademic revolt, rejecting the traditional teaching methods and schools of history painting favored by imperial taste and by many German art academies. The tendency to form secessionist groups became a fundamental characteristic of German artists at the turn of the century. The Munich Secession, whose founding members included Corinth, Slevogt, Uhde, and Wilhelm Trübner, was formed in 1892. The seeds of the Berlin Secession, which first exhibited in 1899, were sown in 1892 with the formation of the Gruppe XI, organized as a protest against the closure of the controversial Edvard Munch exhibition at the Association of Berlin Artists. Munch's paintings, many of which were characterized by a bold two-dimensional style and an introspective symbolism anticipating his Frieze of Life cycle, caused a *succès de scandale.*

Munch, like the Swiss painter Ferdinand Hodler, was represented frequently in exhibitions held in Germany around the turn of the century. The work of both artists appealed to the German taste for idealized allegorical landscapes, a taste which Robert Rosenblum has identified with a "northern romantic tradition." This tradition is also represented by Hans von Marées and Arnold Böcklin, who exercised a strong influence over many German artists working in the late nineteenth century, including Corinth and Modersohn-Becker.

In the first exhibition of the Berlin Secession in 1899 there were works by (among others) Liebermann, Corinth, and Slevogt, who are often grouped together as the leading German impressionist painters, although their borrowings from French impressionism were of a superficial nature. They placed more emphasis on subject matter than did their French counterparts, and, despite their preoccupation with the effects of light, their paintings have little in common with Monet's optical experiments. The free brushwork of many German impressionist canvases probably owes as much to Dutch sources, particularly the work of Frans Hals, as it does to the paintings of contemporary Frenchmen.

Liebermann, Corinth, and Slevogt had all studied in Paris, but within Germany at the turn of the century access to French impressionist and post-impressionist works depended largely on the efforts of the more progressive exhibiting societies, dealers, and critics. Meier-Graefe's writings did much to champion the cause of French art, as did the purchases and exhibitions organized by dealers such as Arnold and Richter in Dresden and Gurlitt and Cassirer in Berlin. Hugo von Tschudi, who became director of the Berlin National Gallery in 1896, encouraged the acquisition of French paintings, purchasing a Cézanne for the gallery as early as 1897. However, his support for French works displeased the state, and he was dismissed from his post in 1908.

Such state opposition, in combination with a physically and theoretically splintered artistic community, the influence of controversial ideas from abroad, and a public whose tastes were often conditioned by provincial insularity, certainly was the cause of that condition in the contemporary artist which Meier-Graefe described as a "confused state of mind."

Max Liebermann   1847–1935

Born in Berlin, Liebermann studied at the Weimar
School of Art between 1869 and 1872. After working in
Paris, Holland, and Munich, he settled in Berlin in
1884. In the 1880s he experimented with
Freilichtmalerei (open-air painting), encouraged by
his visits to Holland and his friendship with the
painter Fritz von Uhde. In 1892 he founded the
Gruppe XI with Walter Leistikow, Herrmann, and
Ludwig von Hofmann as a protest against the closure
of a Munch exhibition at the Association of Berlin
Artists. In the late 1890s he became increasingly
interested in French impressionism and concentrated
on the handling of light and color in his own
paintings. He was one of the founding members of the
Berlin Secession in 1898.

174   *Eva*   1883

sdbr. M. Liebermann 83
95.5 x 67 cm/37 1/2 x 26 1/2 in
Kunsthalle, Hamburg, West Germany
RA 256 *(illustrated in color)*

Ferdinand Hodler   1853–1918

Born in Berne, Hodler began his studies in 1872 at the Ecole des Beaux-Arts, Geneva. In 1885 he held his first one-man show at the Cercle des Beaux-Arts in that city. His work from the mid-1880s onward exhibited an increasing concern with the symbolic representation of the relationship between the rhythms of nature and the rhythm of emotion. In his large friezes from the 1890s Hodler used stylized gestures within flat, decorative designs to suggest a controlled, rhythmic motion. These works place him within the European symbolist and art nouveau movement; he showed in the Paris Salon de la Rose + Croix in 1892 and with the Libre Esthétique, Brussels, in 1901. His paintings were particularly popular in Germany, where he

became a member of the Berlin Secession in 1900 and of the Munich Secession in 1904.

175   *Eurhythmy*   1895

Eurhythmie
sdbr. Ferd. Hodler 1895   167 x 245 cm/
65 3/4 x 96 1/2 in
Kunstmuseum, Bern, Switzerland
RA 250

176   *Lake Geneva from Chexbres*   1895

Genfersee von Chexbres aus
sbr. F. Hodler   100 x 130 cm/39 1/4 x 51 1/4 in
Gottfried Keller Foundation, on loan to the
Kunsthaus, Zurich
RA 251

Lovis Corinth   1858–1925

Born in East Prussia, Corinth received his initial art
training in Königsberg and Munich. During 1884–1886
he studied in Antwerp and Paris, where he worked
with William Adolphe Bouguereau and Fleury at the
Académie Julian. In 1891 he settled in Munich,
becoming a founding member of the Munich
Secession the following year. After moving to Berlin in
1900 he developed a quasi-impressionistic style under
the influence of other *Freilichtmalerei* painters such
as Liebermann and Max Slevogt. He became renowned
for his portrait painting, and between c. 1900 and 1910
he also worked on a series of large figure paintings
based on mythological themes and characterized by
elaborate designs and a profusion of heavy, voluptuous
figures. After a stroke in 1911 he developed a looser,
more emotionally charged style of painting.

177   *Childhood of Zeus*   1905

Die Kindheit des Zeus
sdtl. Lovis Corinth 1905   120 x 150 cm/47 1/4 x 59 in
Kunsthalle, Bremen, West Germany
RA 245

178   *Portrait of Mutter Rosenhagen*   1899

Bildnis Mutter Rosenhagen
sdbr. Lovis Corinth 1899 Nov.   oil on board
63 x 78 cm/24 3/4 x 30 3/4 in
Staatliche Museen Preussischer Kulturbesitz,
Nationalgalerie, Berlin
RA 242

Edvard Munch   1863–1944

Born in Norway, Munch first visited Paris in 1885,
returning there in 1889; he was particularly impressed
with the work of van Gogh, Gauguin, and the
neo-impressionists. During this period Munch
experimented with open-air painting while also
developing a more two-dimensional style reminiscent
of Gauguin's work. In 1892 he went to Berlin where he
exhibited at the Association of Berlin Artists. After a
controversial reception the show was closed, and in
protest a group of painters formed Gruppe XI.
Following this exhibition Munch began work on a
series of paintings for his Frieze of Life cycle, based on
the themes of love and death. These works are
characterized by undulating rhythms, flat color areas,
and disturbing color combinations, reflecting a
personal emotional unease. In autumn 1908 he entered
a clinic in Copenhagen after a nervous collapse,
returning to Norway in 1909.

179   *The Artist's Sister*   1892

Søster Inger
sdbl. E. Munch 1892
172 x 122.5 cm/67 3/4 x 48 1/4 in
Nasjonalgalleriet, Oslo

180 *Moonlight* 1895

Måneskinn
sdbl. E Munch 95
93 x 110 cm/36 3/4 x 43 1/4 in
Nasjonalgalleriet, Oslo

181 *The Dance of Life* 1899/1900

Livets dans
sdbl. E. Munch 99; sdtr. Munch 1900
125.5 x 190.5 cm/49 1/2 x 75 in
Nasjonalgalleriet, Oslo

Otto Modersohn   1865–1943

Born in Soest, Modersohn studied at the Düsseldorf
and Munich Academies during 1884–1888. He was
one of the founding members of the Worpswede
artists' colony in 1889. In the 1890s he painted many
views of Worpswede, in a style influenced by the
Barbizon school and often described as "nature
lyricism" *(Naturlyrismus)*. He exhibited eight of these
landscapes at the International Exhibition in the
Munich Glaspalast in 1895, where they won critical
acclaim. In 1901 he married Paula Becker, with whom
he worked closely in Worpswede during 1902–1903,
developing a more simplified two-dimensional style.
After Modersohn-Becker's premature death in 1907 he
moved to Fischerhude and continued to work,
concentrating on landscapes.

182   *Autumn Morning on the Moor Canal*   1895

Herbstmorgen am Moorkanal
sdbl. Otto Modersohn Worpswede 95
96 x 151 cm/37 3/4 x 59 1/2 in
Bernhard Kaufmann, Haus am Weyerberg,
Worpswede, West Germany
RA 260

Emil Nolde   1867–1956

Nolde was born Emil Hansen in north Schleswig. He
studied in Munich under Adolf Hölzel in 1899 and at
the Académie Julian, Paris, in 1900. His landscapes
from the period c. 1900–1903 have a hazy, atmospheric
quality reminiscent of Hölzel's work and appropriate
to the gray, misty scenery of Nolde's native Schleswig
countryside. Under the influence of Munch and the
French post-impressionists he developed a freer style
with a brighter palette, which appealed to the early
Brücke group. In 1906, the year after his first one-man
show at the Galerie Arnold Dresden, he was invited to
join Die Brücke, but left the group in 1907.

183   *Moonlit Night*   1903

Mondnacht
sbr. Emil Nolde; insc on rev. Mondnacht Emil Nolde
65 x 82.5 cm/25 1/2 x 32 1/2 in
Ludwig Museum, Cologne, West Germany
RA 268

Max Slevogt 1868–1932

Slevogt was based in Munich from 1872. After studying in Munich, Paris, Italy, and Holland, he collaborated on the Jugendstil magazines *Jugend* and *Simplicissimus* in the late 1890s. In 1901 he moved to Berlin where he developed a quasi-impressionistic style, close to that of his Berlin colleagues Corinth and Liebermann. Slevogt's subjects were largely taken from the stage, the opera, and the ballet; perhaps his best known works from this period are his series of paintings of Francesco d'Andrade playing Don Giovanni in Mozart's opera. His interest in an impressionistic treatment of light and color continued and is evident in a group of brightly colored landscapes painted after a trip to Egypt in 1913.

184 *The Champagne Aria from "Don Giovanni"* 1901/1902

Die Champagner-Arie aus "Don Giovanni"
sdbr. Slevogt 1902
105 x 131.5 cm/41 3/4 x 51 3/4 in
Niedersächsische Landesmuseum, Hanover, West Germany
RA 270

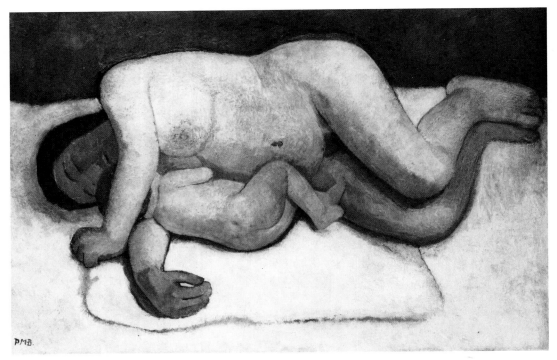

Paula Modersohn-Becker 1876–1907

Paula Becker was born in Dresden, moving to Bremen with her family in 1888. She attended the Berlin School of Art for Women in 1896–1898, after which she settled in the artists' colony of Worpswede and took instruction from the painter Fritz Mackensen. Her early Worpswede works were mostly dark-toned moor scenes and detailed charcoal drawings of local peasant subjects, but after her first trip to Paris in 1900 she began to develop a more simplified, two-dimensional style, seeking what she called "the great simplicity of form." In 1901 she married the Worpswede painter Otto Modersohn. Increasingly dissatisfied with the insular outlook of the colony, she returned to Paris in 1903, 1905, and 1906–1907. In her later work the themes of mother and child or children, which were popular within the Worpswede group, are treated in a style influenced by French post-impressionist sources, particularly the work of Gauguin, van Gogh, and Cézanne.

186   *Reclining Mother and Child*   1906

Mutter und Kind, Liegende Akt
sbl. PMB   82 x 124.5 cm/32 1/4 x 49 in
Collection Ludwig Roselius Sammlung,
Böttcherstrasse, Bremen, West Germany
RA 262

185   *Girl and Boy*   c. 1903

Mädchen und Knabe
sbl. PMB   oil on cardboard
55.5 x 35 cm/21 3/4 x 13 3/4 in
Collection Morton D. May *(not in exhibition)*

187

188

Ernst Ludwig Kirchner 1880–1938

Kirchner studied architecture in Dresden between
1901 and 1904, interrupting this schooling with a
period of art studies in Munich during 1903–1904. In
1905 he formed Die Brücke in Dresden with Erich
Heckel, Karl Schmidt-Rottluff, and Bleyl. His earliest
Brücke paintings are characterized by bright colors
and exaggerated brushwork, a style partly influenced
by van Gogh whose work was exhibited in Dresden in
1905. Kirchner's woodcuts from the same period show
a cruder, more angular technique. After settling in
Berlin with the other Brücke painters in 1911, he
founded the Art School MUIM (Moderner Unterricht
in Malerei) with Max Pechstein.

187   *The Loam Pit*   c. 1906

Die Lehmgrube
sbl. E. L. Kirchner   oil on cardboard on panel
51 x 71 cm/20 x 28 in
Thyssen-Bornemisza Collection, Lugano-
Castagnola, Switzerland
RA 253

188   *Woman in a Birch Wood*   1906

Frau im Birkenwald
ns.   68 x 78 cm/27 x 30 1/2 in
Thyssen-Bornemisza Collection, Lugano-
Castagnola, Switzerland
RA 254

Erich Heckel   1883–1970

In 1904–1905 Heckel studied architecture at the
Technische Hochschule in Dresden, where he met
Kirchner, Bleyl, and Schmidt-Rottluff, with whom he
formed Die Brücke in 1905. His early Brücke paintings
are characterized by broad brushstrokes of strident
color and tense, linear rhythms. In 1911 he settled in
Berlin with the other Brücke artists.

189   *Seated Child*   1906

Sitzendes Kind
sdtl. EH 06   70 x 64 cm/27 1/2 x 25 1/4 in
Brücke-Museum, Berlin
RA 247

cat. no. 193 (detail)

Great Britain

ANNA GRUETZNER

Prior to 1880 Britain supported an independent school of painting that was recognized and admired abroad. Subsequently, following a drastic reevaluation of domestic art, young British painters turned to Paris for their inspiration, adopting instead the styles and techniques of French painting. For this reason, the reverberations of impressionism in the post-impressionist period were as apparent in Britain as they were in France.

British art students went to Paris because they wanted to be up-to-date; but once there, the majority of them never left the Anglo-American circle that dominated the ateliers and artistic colonies in the 1880s. Their knowledge of French painting was restricted to what was shown at the Salon, and they chose to emulate painters who were both accessible and acceptable. Of the Salon painters, Jules Bastien-Lepage had by far the most appeal. By adding sentiment to naturalistic subjects, and combining a highly finished technique with natural light effects, Bastien offered a new interpretation of the peasant paintings of Jean-François Millet, Jules Breton, and Léon Augustin Lhermitte, as well as the landscapes of the Barbizon school, all of which were very widely admired in France and abroad during this period. The similarities of subject and composition evident in the assembled paintings by George Clausen, John Lavery, Walter Osborne, and William Stott attest to the enormous influence that Bastien had on British artists. However, these artists did not belong to one single group, but discovered Bastien's paintings and methods at different times and in different ways: his style was at this date a truly international phenomenon.

Bastien's followers were never the most advanced artistic group in Britain. This mantle fell on the young artists who moved in James McNeill Whistler's circle and later turned to Degas and Monet for inspiration. As artist, aesthetician, and art politician, Whistler was a major force in the development of progressive British painting. His followers Walter Richard Sickert, Sidney Starr, and Théodore Roussel drew great benefit from his insistence on the priority of form over subject. Equally, his belief in the necessity of small, select groups of artists encouraged them when they chose to promote their own aesthetic. These three men and Philip Wilson Steer were all members of a clique

fig. 1   Spencer Gore. *Gauguins and Connoisseurs at the Stafford Gallery.* Private Collection

which emerged as the most progressive faction in British art with its domination of the New English Art Club in 1888. This exhibiting society had been founded in 1886 along the lines of the Paris Salon by French-trained British artists whose work was not receiving its just attention at the Royal Academy. Most of the work shown in the first exhibition was influenced by Bastien, but in 1888 the impressionist artists gained control of the hanging committee and gave places of honor to Steer's and John Singer Sargent's Monet-influenced landscapes and to the Degas-inspired London subjects of Sickert and Starr. Sickert and Sargent in particular had first-hand information from the French—Sickert had been taking informal lessons from Degas, and Sargent knew Monet well. In 1889 the clique strengthened their position when Sickert, Starr, Steer, and Roussel formed part of the group which showed as "The London Impressionists." The sympathetic criticism of George Moore and D. S. MacColl, informal meetings and exhibitions in the artists' studios, and the launching in 1890 of *The Whirlwind*, the organ of impressionism, which published their drawings and criticism, created an atmosphere ripe for experiment. These painters continued to exhibit at the New English Art Club, and the return of Charles Conder, Roger Fry, and William Rothenstein from Paris in the early 1890s added new talent to the Club's ranks.

Although they acknowledged their borrowings from the French, the NEAC clique wanted to produce paintings that were technically advanced but still identifiably English. Sickert, who was influenced by Degas' views about the importance of national art, was especially eager to promote a progressive English school, and his solution was to paint London subjects—in his case music halls. In his preface to *The London*

Impressionists catalogue he prescribed that subjects should be sought within a four-mile radius of London. Also peculiar to these painters was their fascination with the mauve and blue shades of twilight and night. Whistler had set a precedent for this interest, and Stott, Steer, Sickert, Starr, and Rothenstein all attempted to capture the poetic quality of twilight and the mysterious effects of night, so characteristic of the English climate and so different from the sunlit landscapes of France.

By 1894 the movement behind the 1888 takeover had lost its momentum, and the NEAC no longer wanted to acknowledge its connections with radical French art. Instead its members turned to eighteenth-century themes and looked to the landscape style of John Constable and Jean-Baptiste-Camille Corot. Sickert was the exception to this new trend, but he soon retreated to Dieppe where he was to remain until 1905. The decision to return to a more English style came just at the moment when the paintings of Gauguin, van Gogh, and Cézanne might have found acceptance and approval. There was no lack of knowledge about these artists among the better informed, and the Pont-Aven paintings of Roderic O'Conor and Forbes-Robertson show that the British did respond to the work of French artists when painting away from the pressures of the London art scene. However, in London, the general opinion was that French painting had had a detrimental effect on British art and had encouraged facile, derivative works. This sudden aversion to French influence and the desire to reestablish an independent English school was so strong that there was little exchange with France until 1905.

After 1905, a new group of young painters under Sickert's guidance took up where the older generation had left off. In 1910 Roger Fry's *Manet and the Post-Impressionists* exhibition, which showed paintings by Gauguin, van Gogh, and Cézanne, renewed English interest in French art, and there followed a spate of exhibitions in London which did much to foster English modernism. Spencer Gore's *Gauguins and Connoisseurs at the Stafford Gallery* (1911–1912, fig. 1) stands as a token of the enthusiastic reception post-impressionist painting had in England at that time, in a second wave of French influence which lies beyond the terminal date of the present exhibition.

Théodore Roussel   1847–1926

Born in Brittany, Roussel settled in London in c. 1874
and became a follower of Whistler in 1885. He was one
of the progressive clique at the New English Art Club
and showed with the London Impressionists in 1889,
but his paintings of Chelsea and the Thames remained
closer to Whistler's work than those of the other
followers. Concerned with the accurate representation
of the colors of nature, Roussel invented a scientific
method for determining proper tonal relationships.
His paintings of the nude out-of-doors or in
contemporary settings achieved notoriety because the
subject was still taboo in academic circles in England
during the 1880s.

190   *The Bathers*   1887

ns.   39.5 x 29 cm/15 1/2 x 11 1/2 in
Guy Roussel, the Artist's Grandson
RA 331

George Clausen 1852–1944

Seeing Bastien-Lepage's paintings and meeting him in London in 1880 prompted Clausen to abandon his paintings of Dutch subjects and Whistler-inspired portraits and move to the English countryside to paint the peasantry. A trip to Brittany in 1882 gave him an opportunity to paint similar subjects in France. Clausen was much criticized in the 1880s for his dependence on Bastien-Lepage's style with its high horizon line, flattened space, and meticulous natural detail painted over a thinly washed background. A founding member of the New English Art Club, Clausen rose to these attacks, stressing the need for British painters to learn from French art. In the 1890s he adopted more inventive figure compositions and a brighter palette, under the influence of French impressionism.

191   *Haytime*   1882

  sdbr. G. Clausen 1882   68.5 x 60 cm/27 x 23 3/4 in
  Art Gallery of Ontario, Toronto, Purchase 1937

192   *Peasant Girl Carrying a Jar, Quimperlé*   1882

  sdbr and insc. G. Clausen 1882 Quimperlé
  46 x 27.5 cm/18 x 10 3/4 in
  The Victoria and Albert Museum, London
  RA 280

John Lavery 1856–1941

After seeing Manet's paintings in Paris, Lavery became
interested in subjects from modern life. Two main
preoccupations of the 1880s were summer leisure
activities and the crowded grounds and pavilions of
the Glasgow International Exhibition in 1888. During
this period Lavery was also influenced by
Bastien-Lepage, whose compositions, with their
abrupt changes between planes, were imitated by
Lavery to convey the effect of movement. Later his
paintings became more like those of Whistler, and he
made his reputation with Whistlerian portraits. He
was instrumental in the formation of the International
Society, of which he became vice president under
Whistler.

193 *The Tennis Party* 1885

sdbl. J. Lavery 1885 77 x 183.5 cm/30 1/4 x 69 1/2 in
Aberdeen Art Gallery, Scotland
RA 317

Sidney Starr   1857–1925

A follower of Whistler from the early 1880s, Starr painted a number of Whistlerian portraits and seascapes. Around 1888 this influence was superseded by that of Degas, when Sickert introduced Starr to his methods. Of the painters who showed with the London Impressionists in 1889, Starr was the most heedful of Sickert's plea for London subjects, depicting its streets and suburbs from unusual viewpoints. Starr was adept with pastels and used a similar scratchy technique in his oil paintings. He showed at the New English Art Club from 1888 until 1892, when a scandal forced him to leave for America.

194   *At the Café Royal*   1888

sbl. Starr   pastel on canvas   60 x 50 cm/
23 1/2 x 19 1/2 in
Private Collection
RA 343

195   *A City Atlas*   1888/1889

sbr. Starr   61 x 51 cm/24 x 20 in
National Gallery of Canada, Ottawa
RA 344

William Stott   1857–1900

Stott of Oldham, as he is generally known, enrolled at
the Ecole des Beaux-Arts in 1879. He spent the
summer months at Gretz-sur-Loing, whose picturesque
bridge was frequently painted by British and
American artists in the 1880s. The work of Bastien-
Lepage provided a basis for Stott's open-air painting,
while Jean Charles Cazin and Whistler's canvases
inspired the flat, simplified forms and the thin washes
of paint of his later, poetically conceived, large
landscapes. These had considerable success at the
Salon after 1882. Stott's reputation reached its height
in Paris in 1889 when he had a one-man exhibition at
Durand-Ruel's gallery. In the 1890s he adopted
mythological subjects and a more highly finished
technique.

196   *Girl in a Meadow*   1880

> sdbl. W. Stott 1880   72 x 57.5 cm/28 1/4 x 22 3/4 in
> The Trustees of the Tate Gallery, London
> RA 352

197   *The Two Sisters*   1882

> sdbl. William Stott of Oldham 1882 [William?] Stott
> 189[0?]
> 142 x 216 cm/56 x 85 in
> Rochdale Art Gallery, England
> RA 353

Walter Osborne   1859–1902

Born in Ireland, Osborne studied at the Antwerp
Academy in 1881–1882 before going to Brittany in
1883, where he learned of Bastien-Lepage's technique
from its practitioners there. In the 1880s he made
several painting trips to popular spots such as
Walberswick in Suffolk, where he met Philip Wilson
Steer. Like many of Bastien's followers, Osborne used
his methods as a basis for experiments with brighter
colors and freer techniques.

198   *An October Morning*   1885

sdbl. Walter Osborne 1885[?]   71 x 91.5 cm/28 x 36 in
Guildhall Art Gallery, London
RA 327

Roderic O'Conor   1860–1940

O'Conor went to Paris in 1883 and, except for short periods, never left France again. His thickly encrusted paint surfaces of the early 1890s, with their diagonal strokes of pure color, were probably influenced by van Gogh whose paintings he could have seen when they both showed at the Indépendants in 1890. His decorative treatment of forms and his metaphysical preoccupations, however, bring him closer to the Pont-Aven artists with whom he was on friendly terms. After his meeting in 1894 with Gauguin, who wanted O'Conor to accompany him to Tahiti in 1895, his work approached Gauguin's style for a short while. After 1900 he was an important figure in the Anglo-Saxon circle in Paris, at which time his work had affinities with fauvism.

199   *Breton Peasant Woman Knitting*   1893

> sdtl. O'Conor 1893   oil on board
> 81.5 x 68 cm/32 x 26 3/4 in
> Mr. and Mrs. George Szpiro, London
> RA 323

200   *The Lezaver Farm, Finistère*   1894

> *La Ferme Lezaver, Finistère*
> sdbl. O'Conor 1894   72 x 93 cm/28 1/2 x 36 1/2 in
> National Gallery of Ireland, Dublin
> RA 324

Walter Richard Sickert   1860–1942

After enrolling at the Slade School of Art in 1881–1882 Sickert became Whistler's pupil. He met Degas in Paris in 1883, and their second meeting at Dieppe in 1885 instigated a lifelong friendship. Degas' example inspired Sickert to concentrate on draftsmanship and compositional structure and encouraged him to paint modern urban subjects — the circus, the racecourse, and the London music hall. He was an active protagonist on behalf of British art and a leader of the progressive faction at the New English Art Club in the 1880s, a role which he repeated with the Fitzroy Street Group in 1907 and the Camden Town Group in 1911, after his return to London from Dieppe. He favored a subdued tonal palette, extending its range to include accents of bright color. In the 1890s he abandoned the spatially complex compositions of his early music hall paintings in favor of a flatter, more decorative handling of form and color.

201   *The Circus*   c. 1885

sbr. Sickert   oil on panel   21.5 x 35.6 cm
8 1/2 x 14 in
Private Collection
RA 334

202   *The October Sun*   c. 1888

ns.   oil on panel   26.5 x 35.5 cm/10 1/2 x 14 in
Castle Museum of Art, Archaeology and Natural
History, Norwich, England
RA 336

203

204

205

203 *Little Dot Hetherington at the Old Bedford Music Hall* 1888/1889

sbr. Sickert   61 x 61 cm/24 x 24 in
Private Collection

204 *The Old Bedford: Cupid in the Gallery*   1890

sbr. Sickert   127 x 77.5 cm/50 x 30 1/2 in
National Gallery of Canada, Ottawa

205 *L'Hôtel Royal, Dieppe*   c. 1894

sbr. Sickert   50 x 61 cm/19 3/4 x 24 in
Private Collection
RA 338 *(illustrated in color)*

206

208

207

Philip Wilson Steer   1860–1942

Steer studied in Paris at the Académie Julian in 1882–1883 and at the Ecole des Beaux-Arts in 1883–1884. On his return to England he produced Whistlerian paintings. His friendship with Sickert and George Moore, which began in 1885, encouraged him to look at impressionist paintings, and from summer 1886 he employed the techniques of Monet and the neo-impressionists in a sequence of brightly colored seascapes figured with young girls or children. These paintings helped to make the New English Art Club a focus for impressionism between 1887 and 1894 and established Steer as one of the most advanced London impressionists. The naïveté of his seaside figures contrasts with a series of formally composed portraits of a model, Rosie Pettigrew, executed in the same period. After 1894 Steer's critics persuaded him to abandon his interest in radical French art, and his

later paintings show connections with eighteenth-century English portraiture and the landscapes of Constable.

206   *Boulogne Sands*   1888/1894

sdbl. P. W. Steer 92   61 x 76 cm/24 x 30 in
The Trustees of the Tate Gallery, London
RA 347 *(illustrated in color)*

207   *Girls Running*   1888/1894

sdbr. P. W. Steer 94   63 x 92.5 cm/24 3/4 x 36 1/2 in
The Trustees of the Tate Gallery, London

208   *The Ermine Sea*   1890

sdbl. P. W. Steer 90   61 x 76 cm/24 x 30 in
Collection Mrs. Anthony Bamford
RA 349

Eric Forbes-Robertson   1865–1935

Forbes-Robertson went to Pont-Aven in 1890, and by
1891 he was moving in the circle of the so-called
Pont-Aven School. His dependence on Gauguin grew
stronger after their meeting in 1894, but the moody,
mysterious quality of his paintings suggests the
interests of Séguin and Alfred Jarry, who were his
closest friends. He contributed to several symbolist
periodicals in Paris before his return to England in
1900.

209   *Great Expectations*   1894

 sdbl and insc. Eric Forbes-Robertson Pont-Aven 94
 75 x 100.5 cm/29 1/2 x 39 1/2 in
 Northampton Art Gallery, England
 RA 289

Roger Fry 1866–1934

After studying science at Cambridge, Fry went to Paris in 1891 and enrolled at the Académie Julian. He moved in the Anquetin/Rothenstein circle and learned the theories of progressive French art. On his return to England, he painted landscapes using flat arabesques and sinuous forms. He was persuaded to abandon this style by the increasingly conservative New English Art Club circle and adopted a more "archaic" manner. He later referred to his early, radical work as "essentially Post-Impressionist" — a phrase that he coined to describe two exhibitions of French art which he organized in London in 1910 and 1912. He made his reputation principally as an art critic and theorist.

210 *Blythborough, the Estuary* 1892/1893

ns. 61 x 74 cm/24 x 29 in
Collection Mrs. Pamela Diamand
RA 290

Charles Conder 1868–1909

After painting open-air landscapes in Australia, where he spent seven years of his youth, Conder went to Paris in 1890 to study at the Académie Julian and was befriended by Anquetin, Toulouse-Lautrec, and Rothenstein. He frequently made trips to paint in the French countryside. Seeing Monet's Haystacks in 1891 inspired his vibrant, light-toned paintings of flowering trees, but his flat, decorative treatment of the landscape owes more to the work of Puvis de Chavannes and Whistler. Conder showed at the New English Art Club from 1893; his delicate treatment of eighteenth-century themes had a great influence on the direction of English painting. In 1894 he moved to London but returned to France frequently.

211 *Blossom at Dennemont* 1893

sdbr and insc. Charles Conder Dennemont. 93
73 x 60 cm/28 3/4 x 23 1/2 in
The Visitors of the Ashmolean Museum, Oxford, England
RA 283

William Rothenstein   1872–1945

While studying at the Académie Julian in Paris,
Rothenstein mixed with a wide circle of artists
including Anquetin and Toulouse-Lautrec. He met
Degas in 1892, after Degas had seen the exhibition of
work by Rothenstein and Conder mounted by Père
Thomas. Degas was to influence him greatly,
particularly through his insistence on the importance
of draftsmanship. It was Degas who persuaded
Rothenstein to return to England in 1894; there he
caused a considerable stir at the New English Art Club
by using flattened, simplified forms in his treatment of
English themes.

212   *Coster Girls*   1894

sdbl. W. R. 94
96.5 x 70 cm/38 x 27 1/2 in
Graves Art Gallery, Sheffield, England

cat. no. 214 (right side)

Italy

SANDRA BERRESFORD

Italian divisionism, like French neo-impressionism, was indebted to recent developments in optical theory, notably to those of O. N. Rood, published in 1879. Rood affirmed that a color mixed on the palette from two other colors was seventy times less luminous than the same color obtained by juxtaposing (or "dividing") the two colors concerned, allowing for their optical fusion at a given distance. Yet, despite this common basis, the French and Italian movements developed independently of each other. Both aimed to explore the phenomena of light and color, but in general, the Italians applied color theory less systematically to their work and obtained radically different results.

Divisionism was originally a Lombard-Piedmontese movement, centered in Milan in the 1890s. Its principal exponents, with the exception of Gaetano Previati and Emilio Longoni, are represented here. A separate, short-lived divisionist (vibrationist) movement under the leadership of Plinio Nomellini grew up in Florence in about 1890–1892. This faction consisted of a group of Giovanni Fattori's pupils who were introduced to aspects of late impressionism by Alfredo Müller. Divisionism later spread to Rome and, in various forms, to all of Italy's provincial artistic centers. It was of fundamental importance in the formation of the futurists, particularly to the work of Giacomo Balla and Umberto Boccioni. A weakened, distorted version, often tainted by nationalistic rhetoric, flourished into the 1920s.

Unlike neo-impressionism, divisionism was not grounded on the discoveries of impressionism since, in Italy, knowledge of the French movement was partial and superficial, even in Florence which could best claim to have maintained ties with Paris in the nineteenth century. There, in 1880, Diego Martelli recognized that impressionism was "not only a revolution in the field of ideas, but a physiological revolution of the human eye," but his was a voice crying in the wilderness, echoed valiantly by that of Vittorio Pica in the following decade. In general, when Italian artists visited Paris in the nineteenth century they were attracted there by the Barbizon school, as well as by the work of Millet and Bastien-Lepage. The term "neo-impressionist" applied to Italian divisionism is anomalous, therefore, and the French movement did not have a direct influence on the Italian divisionists.

The formation of the divisionist movement was influenced instead by two important Italian groups: the scapigliati in Milan and the macchiaioli in Florence. In the 1860s and 1870s, both had tried to

fig. 1 Segantini. *The Two Mothers.*
Civica Galleria d'Arte Moderna, Milan

capture light and atmosphere in their works: the former through lack of contour and use of pale *sfumature* (nuances), the latter through heightened tonal contrasts in open-air landscape sketches. Onto this scapigliati experience the northern divisionists grafted their knowledge of optical texts. Working in relative isolation, each developed a highly original style; only Angelo Morbelli and Giuseppe Pellizza de Volpedo in the early 1890s briefly exhibited technical similarities.

Whatever their unique qualities, all divisionist techniques used divided touches or strokes of contrasting color to represent light. Vittore Grubicy de Dragon saw this technique as the instrument of a new modern aesthetic, a language which introduced "greater social breadth" to art by the depiction of light, which he believed was a manifestation of life. The divisionists applied this concern with light and life to subjects of two kinds: symbolic and pantheistic themes such as those of Giovanni Segantini, which seek visual forms for timeless values; and social and political subjects. In the 1890s the scientific nature of the divisionist technique was closely identified with a positivist-inspired belief in the irrepressible progress of the working classes. Most of the divisionists, like their neo-impressionist counterparts, were committed to social reform to some degree.

A variety of techniques and subject matter were already present in the first exhibited divisionist works, which were shown at the Milan Triennale in 1891. Segantini's *Two Mothers* (fig. 1), a simple symbolic analogy between mother and child and cow and calf, was primarily concerned with portraying nature, in contrast to the symbolist ideal of Previati's *Motherhood* (fig. 2). Longoni's *Strike Orator*, on the other hand, made a social comment. With these works, the divisionists posed basic questions about the artist's role in society. Ironically they, themselves, found these questions unanswerable, failing to resolve the dichotomy in their own art between their interest in symbolism and their social commitment.

Divisionism can only be fully understood within an Italian context. Nevertheless, the divisionists were more open than most of their Italian contemporaries to contacts with other parts of Europe, although (with the exception of Grubicy) they traveled little. Grubicy maintained

fig. 2   Previati. *Motherhood*
Banca Popolare, Novara

contacts with Belgium through *L'Art moderne* and the Libre Esthétique
and assisted Segantini to exhibit at Les XX and Previati to show at the
Salon de la Rose + Croix. All were interested in pre-Raphaelitism and its
later aesthetic developments. Segantini corresponded with leading
German and Austrian artistic figures and was a member of the Vienna
Secession. Morbelli, Pellizza, and notably Segantini exhibited in major
European exhibitions and won international recognition. These artists
fully deserve the label "post-impressionists," since they, like their French
counterparts, were seeking a modern pictorial means of expression
through a radically new exploration of content and technique.

Giovanni Boldini 1842-1931

Born in Ferrara, Boldini joined the macchiaioli in
Florence in 1862. On visits to Paris from 1867 onward,
he met Manet, Degas, Gustave Caillebotte, and Sisley.
Though he kept a house in Paris, he painted in Italy,
Holland, Germany, Spain, and London, and built a
great reputation as a painter of genre scenes and
particularly of society portraits. These he treated with
bold, virtuoso brushstrokes which are partially
indebted to Frans Hals as well as to the art of the
English eighteenth century. Boldini was friendly with
his rivals in portraiture, Sargent, Paul Helleu, and
Whistler, and his house in Paris was frequented by
celebrities such as Sarah Bernhardt, Yvette Guilbert,
and Robert de Montesquiou.

213 *Portrait of Mme. Max* 1896

Portrait de Mme. Max
sdbl. Boldini 1896 200 x 100 cm/78 3/4 x 39 1/2 in
Musée d'Orsay, Paris
RA 364

Vittore Grubicy de Dragon 1851–1920

Grubicy had great importance as a critic, dealer, and propagandist of divisionism. Between 1870 and 1889 he traveled widely in Europe, developing contacts particularly with artists in the Low Countries. Although he knew Fénéon's writings on neo-impressionism, his personal experience of that style was minimal. In his own work he applied tiny flecks of paint over a foundation of dark and light forms. Dominant colors were pale orange, green, blue, and white; the combination of these hues often resulted in a brownish tonality which, like his subject matter, owes much to Millet and the Barbizon school. His later compositions reflect Japanese influence. His small, poetic landscapes, intended to capture the fleeting moods of nature, were the results of a long contemplative process. Many of these landscapes were combined in polyptychs suggestive of his religious, almost mystical response to nature.

214 Triptych: (left) *From the Window, Miazzina* (center) *What Peace in Valganna!* (right) *Summer on Lake Como*   c. 1894/1901

(left) *Dalla Finestra, Miazzina* (center) *Che Pace in Valganna!* (right) *Estate sul Lago di Como* Galleria Nazionale d'Arte Moderna, Rome

(left) *From The Window, Miazzina*   1898

s and insc br. Dalla finestra, Miazzina Grubicy 47.5 x 39 cm/18 3/4 x 15 1/2 in

(center) *What Peace in Valganna!*   c. 1894

sbr. V. Grubicy   36.5 x 62 cm/14 1/4 x 24 1/2 in

(right) *Summer on Lake Como*   1897/1901

sbl. V. Grubicy   48 x 40 cm/19 x 15 3/4 in
RA 368

Angelo Morbelli   1853–1919

Encouraged by Vittore Grubicy, Morbelli turned toward divisionism in the late 1880s. He evolved the technique from his own experimentation and through an increasing interest in optical texts. Of all the divisionists, he was the most rigorous in applying color theories to his work. First, he sketched out his painting in terms of chiaroscuro on a neutral ground; then he created his vibrating, luminous surfaces by applying pure color in a network of fine, short brushstrokes, using a hard, three-pointed brush which he devised for this purpose. Interested in contemporary social problems, Morbelli avoided the symbolist/idealistic convictions of many of his fellow divisionists. Most of his works after 1883 depict the old people of Pio Luogo Trivulzio, Milan, whom he portrayed with a dispassionate yet sympathetic vision.

215   *The First Letter*   1890

La Prima Lettera
sdbl. Morbelli 1890   104 x 78 cm/41 x 30 3/4 in
Private Collection
RA 369

216   *For Eighty Cents*   1895

Per Ottanta Centesimi
sdbr. Morbelli 1895   70 x 124 cm/27 1/2 x 48 3/4 in
Civico Museo Antonio Borgogna, Vercelli, Italy
RA 370   *(illustrated in color)*

217   *The Christmas of Those Left Behind*   1903

Il Natale dei Rimasti
sdbr. A. Morbelli 1903   59 x 104 cm/23 1/4 x 41 in
Galleria d'Arte Moderna, Venice
RA 371

Giovanni Segantini   1858–1899

The most famous of the divisionists, Segantini exhibited throughout Europe and was especially popular in Germany, Austria, and Switzerland. He evolved his highly individual technique during the 1880s; the repainting of *Ave Maria a Trasbordo* in 1886 at Grubicy's suggestion was a landmark in this development. In his paintings he used a red/brown ground, superimposing heavy layers of pigment in directional brushstrokes used to create volume. The resultant strawlike effect owes more to Ruskin's teachings and Millet's pastels than to optical theories received secondhand from Grubicy. Red and green are the only complementaries consistently superimposed. Segantini considered his pastoral idylls to be expressions of "naturalist symbolism," reflecting his inherent pantheism, but they also belong to the tradition of European naturalism running from the Barbizon school and Millet to Bastien-Lepage. Other

works, inspired by literary sources and pre-Raphaelite models, fit into the mainstream of European symbolism. Segantini never fully resolved this essential conflict between the real and the spiritual.

218   *Rest in the Shade*   1892

Riposo all'ombra
sdbr. G. Segantini 92   44 x 68 cm/17 1/2 x 26 3/4 in
Gesellschaft Kruppsche Gemäldesammlung, Essen, West Germany
RA 382

219   *Love at the Source of Life* or *The Fountain of Youth*   1896

Amore alla Fonte della Vita or *La Fontana della Giovinezza*
sdbr. G. Segantini Maloja 1896
75 x 100 cm/29 1/2 x 39 1/2 in
Civica Galleria d'Arte Moderna, Milan
RA 383

220 *The Representation of Spring*   1897

La Raffigurazione della Primavera
sdbl. G. Segantini 1897
116 x 227 cm/45 1/2 x 89 1/2 in
The Fine Arts Museums of San Francisco,
Jacob Stern Permanent Loan Collection
RA 384

Plinio Nomellini   1866–1943

Nomellini studied with Giovanni Fattori in Florence in the late 1880s and was initially influenced by the macchiaioli. His divisionist technique evolved against a background of nominal impressionist influence in Florence and thus stems from a different context from that of his northern counterparts. He met them through Pellizza with whom he shared an interest in social reform. Nomellini's paintings are freely handled and immediate responses to nature. Pure colors are used inconsistently and are mixed with white in an impressionist fashion; there is none of Morbelli's scientific rigor. After 1900, Nomellini reverted to a generic impressionism, comparable to that of Besnard in France or Liebermann in Germany, exploring the portrayal of light in terms of color.

221   *The First Reading Lesson* c. 1905

Prime Letture
sbr. Plinio Nomellini
167 x 167 cm/65 3/4 x 65 3/4 in
Civica Galleria d'Arte Moderna, Milan
RA 373

Giuseppe Pellizza da Volpedo   1868–1907

Pellizza was one of the masters of divisionism. He first experimented in the technique around 1892, encouraged by Nomellini. His correspondence with Morbelli after 1894 traces his methodical efforts to inform himself not only about optical theories, which he applied to his work, but also about the social question. Possibly influenced by the writings of Charles Blanc and Charles Henry, he was the only divisionist to draw any general conclusions about the psychological implications of form, line, and color. Pellizza treated a wide range of subjects: idyllic naturalism with symbolist overtones; the committed, if idealized, socialism of *The Fourth Estate;* portraits; and landscapes. He gradually abandoned symbolism and humanitarian themes after 1900, to concentrate on landscape and on a more radical analysis of light,

notably in his series depicting the sun's rays. He killed himself in 1907.

222   *The Procession*   1892/1896

La Processione
scr. [on stone by river] Pellizza
86 x 158 cm/34 x 73 in
Museo Nazionale della Scienza e Tecnica, Milan
RA 374

223   *The Mirror of Life (That Which the First One Does, the Others Follow)*   1895/1898

Lo Specchio della Vita (E cio che fa la prima, e l'altre fanno)
sdbc. [on painted frame] Pellizza   1895-98
center panel   87 x 200 cm/34 1/4 x 78 3/4 in;
total   132 x 291 cm/52 x 114 3/4 in
Civica Galleria d'Arte Moderna, Turin, Italy
RA 375

224   *The Fourth Estate*   1901

Il Quarto Stato
sdcr. [on top of wall] P. di Volpedo 1901
283 x 550 cm/111 3/4 x 206 3/4 in
Civica Galleria d'Arte Moderna, Milan
RA 376 *(illustrated in color)*

225   *Washing in the Sun*   1905

Panni al Sole
sdbr. G. Pellizza 1905   87 x 131 cm/34 1/4 x 51 3/4 in
Private Collection
RA 377

Giacomo Balla   1871–1958

Balla's first divisionist painting was executed in Rome in 1897, influenced by knowledge of works by Pellizza and Morbelli. He practiced divisionism with confidence after 1902 in portraits, industrial landscapes, and works demonstrating his social concern. Balla's divisionism was essentially empirical, not scientific: he applied pure color onto the canvas without seeking the juxtaposition of complementaries. This procedure resulted in a lively, expressive, and at times, graphic pictorial surface. He used the technique to study the phenomenon of natural and artificial light and considered it the most suitable language in which to express his commitment to subjects from modern life. The abstract, decorative

potential of this style formed the basis of his first futurist experiments, the *Iridescent Interpenetrations* of 1912.

226   *Self-Portrait*   1902

Autoritratto
sbc. Balla; sdtr. Balla 1902   58 x 43.5 cm/
23 x 17 1/4 in
Private Collection
RA 358

227   *Portrait in the Open Air*   1902/1903

Ritratto all'Aperto
sbr. Balla 154.4 x 113 cm/60 3/4 x 44 1/4 in
Galleria Nazionale d'Arte Moderna, Rome
RA 359

Umberto Boccioni 1882–1916

Of all the futurist painters, Boccioni was the most
deeply affected by divisionism. He was directed
toward the technique by Balla, whose influence is
evident in the solidity and immediacy of Boccioni's
first portraits, in their strong tonal oppositions, and in
the graphic quality of his divisionist touch. Balla also
led him to pure colors and subjects from modern life,
seen particularly in his industrial landscapes after
1908. Under Previati's influence, Boccioni toyed with
symbolism for a brief period between 1908 and 1910.
He took the expressive qualities of Previati's style as
well as his scientific usage of color and combined
them with Balla's plasticity and sense of form to create
the basis of his early futurist style.

228 *La Signora Virginia* 1905

sdbr and insc. U. Boccioni Roma giugno 1905
140 x 115.5 cm/55 x 45 1/2 in
Civica Galleria d'Arte Moderna, Milan
RA 362

cat. no. 235

The Low Countries

MARYANNE STEVENS

A younger generation rising in defiance of a ruling artistic establishment was no novel event in the history of nineteenth-century painting. Yet, during the early 1880s, Belgium and Holland witnessed an extreme example of defiance, one expressed with such intensity that it determined the pattern of art over the subsequent twenty-five years. In so doing, it gave birth to a number of artistic and literary institutions committed to innovation, as well as heralding a period of intense individual and group experimentation in art.

The artistic institution which epitomized this defiance, the Sint Lukas Society, was founded in Amsterdam in 1880. This society was formed by a group of young artists whose challenge to the State Art Academy was made in two ways: by adopting the nonacademic, painterly style of the Hague School and by placing art within the broader context of music, literature, and drama through the organization of lectures and discussions. Three years later, a similar group arose in Brussels. On 28 October 1883, twenty Belgian artists, outraged at the rejection of their works by the official Salon, gathered at the Taverne Guillaume to found an alternative exhibiting body. Calling themselves "The Twenty," or "Les XX," they agreed to hold annual spring exhibitions bound by no aesthetic doctrine and open, through invitation, to progressive artists working in both Belgium and abroad. Each exhibition was to be complemented by lectures, concerts, poetry and play readings in the exhibition galleries. Despite organizational changes in 1893, when the group was rechristened "La Libre Esthétique," its policy of inviting artists from Europe as well as America made this organization one of the centers of avant-garde art during the period.

The range of experimentation introduced by such international exhibitions seems at first glance to have stimulated myriad individual styles in the Low Countries. Yet the artists all shared two features in common, the desire to make painting more than merely representational and a resort to similar visual sources to achieve this end. In keeping with artists elsewhere in Europe, the painters of the Low Countries wished to advance beyond the requirement that painting should create an accurate, realistic record of the external world. Instead they sought to make their art the vehicle for ideas and emotions. James Ensor's *Russian Music*, 1881 (fig. 1), while depicting a domestic interior, conveys deeper, underlying emotions by overlaying the image with a dense network of

fig. 1   Ensor. *Russian Music.*
Musées Royaux des Beaux-Arts de
Belgique, Brussels

colors and brushstrokes. Similarly, Jan Toorop's reduction of neo-impressionism to a decorative pattern of dots illustrates his manipulation of a naturalistic technique for nonnaturalistic ends.

In their search for new, nonrepresentational styles, the artists of the Low Countries rediscovered their own indigenous colorist tradition and turned to the paintings of the French avant-garde. Les XX, in Brussels, enthusiastically adopted contemporary progressive art from Paris, to which they had access through their annual exhibitions. In 1887, the group saw neo-impressionist paintings by Seurat; in the following year, several Belgian artists, including Henri van de Velde and Théo van Rysselberghe, and one Dutch artist, Toorop, were converted to the style. That same year the new style of pictorial symbolism, represented by the work of Anquetin, had its first exposition at Les XX. Reinforced during the next five years by the work of Gauguin, Bernard, Denis, van Gogh, and Toulouse-Lautrec, the impact of symbolism can be seen in the paintings of Toorop made around 1890 and in the canvases of Johannes Thorn Prikker. Finally, Whistler, an adopted member of the Paris avant-garde, was invited to exhibit at Les XX in 1884, 1886, and 1888, and the influence of his portraits and his formal organization of color can be seen in the work of Fernand Khnopff and Toorop in the mid-1880s.

Another French source adopted by some artists in Belgium and Holland was the Barbizon school. Although belonging to the mid-nineteenth century, these landscape painters, including Charles-François Daubigny, Narciso Diaz de la Peña, and Théodore Rousseau, had defied traditional French interpretations of landscape by their gross, almost crude handling of thick impasto. For artists of the Low Countries, this technique of painting reinforced currents already present in their own heritage. Thus, when Ensor began to build up his heavily laden picture surfaces, he was responsive both to the Barbizon school and to the Flemish colorist tradition, exemplified by Peter Paul Rubens and perpetuated in the nineteenth century by artists such as Boulenger, Braekelaer, and Artan de Saint-Martin. Similarly, in Holland, the Hague School of painters led by Hendrik Mesdag, Jozef Israels, and Anton Mauve was indebted to the Dutch seventeenth-century painting tradition and to the exhibition of Barbizon paintings held in 1882 in The Hague. The effect of this fusion can be seen in the emphasis on color and surface texture in the work of Georg-Hendrik Breitner, Floris-Hendrik Verster, and Willem Witsen.

The impact of external avant-garde sources persisted in Brussels. The assimilation of the political and artistic ideas of William Morris and the English Arts and Crafts movement and the flat, decorative work of the Paris symbolists was seminal in forging the art nouveau style, of which Henri van de Velde became a leading exponent after 1892. The two-way link with Paris was sealed in 1892 when Paul Signac became a member of Les XX, and in 1897 when van Rysselberghe settled in Paris. The continuing desire to exhibit the most recent developments in art also brought invitations in 1906 to Charles Camoin, Albert Marquet, Matisse, and Maillol to show at the Libre Esthétique.

The response of Holland after c. 1890 to outside influences was the reverse of that of Belgium. After the brief impact of Les XX on The Hague in the early 1890s, a period of isolationism seems to have begun. An international exhibition of recent French and Belgian art, including three paintings by van Gogh and four by Cézanne, held in The Hague in 1901 passed virtually unnoticed. Similar reactions were recorded to exhibitions held in Amsterdam between 1901 and 1905, which included works by Monet, Renoir, Camille Pissarro, Toorop, and van Gogh. Yet, despite this retreat into more personal modes of expression, it is important to note, that Piet Mondrian emerged in c. 1901 from this provincial, crepuscular school of Amsterdam painting to become a leading exponent of abstract art in the twentieth century.[1]

[1]This essay is indebted in part to Joop Joostens' essay, "Painting in Holland," published in the catalogue of the exhibition at the Royal Academy of Arts, *Post-Impressionism, Cross-Currents in European Painting*, London, 1979.

Georg-Hendrick Breitner   1857–1923

Breitner was born in Rotterdam. His artistic
development was most strongly influenced by his
study with two leading members of the Hague School,
Mesdag and Willem Maris, and by his experiences at
the Atelier Cormon in Paris, where he met
Toulouse-Lautrec, Bernard, and Anquetin. Although
he moved to Amsterdam in 1886, Breitner continued
to paint his pictures of contemporary life in the
brighter palette adopted by the Hague School during
the 1880s. By about 1892, however, while still
retaining the school's loose technique and heavily
loaded paint surfaces, Breitner began to adopt
crepuscular tones which reflected both his interest in
photography and his association with leading
Amsterdam artists such as Witsen. He exhibited at
Les XX in 1886 and 1889.

229   *Lauriergracht, Amsterdam*   c. 1895

sbr. G. H. Breitner   76 x 116 cm/30 x 45 3/4 in
Stedelijk Museum, Amsterdam, Gift of the
Vereeniging tot het vormen van een Openbare
Verzameling van Hedendaagse Kunst, 1949
RA 389

Fernand Khnopff   1858–1921

Born in Bruges, where he first trained, Khnopff
completed his studies in Paris. He settled in Brussels
and after 1900 became a virtual recluse. His art
summarizes a number of different influences and
interests. As a founding member of Les XX, he
absorbed the formal organization and almost
monochromatic palette of Whistler's portraits shown
at the group's exhibitions. His friendships with
symbolist writers such as Grégoire Le Roy, Verhaeren,
and Maurice Maeterlinck may have informed the
introspective, suggestive aspect of his art, while his
fascination with decorative surfaces and wistful,
unattainable women derived from his admiration of
the English pre-Raphaelites, especially Dante Gabriel
Rossetti and Edward Burne-Jones.

230   *Roses and Japanese Fan*   c. 1885

Roses et éventail japonais
sbr. Fernand Khnopff   50 x 25 cm/19 3/4 x 9 3/4 in
Collection Marcel Mabille, Brussels
RA 404

231   *Portrait of Madame Van Ryckevorsel*   1888

Portrait de Madame Van Ryckevorsel
sbl. Fernand Khnopff   oil on panel
47 x 36 cm/18 1/2 x 14 1/4 in
Private Collection
RA 403

232   *Portrait of Jeanne de Bauer*   1890

Portrait de Jeanne de Bauer
sbl. Fernand Khnopff   51 x 33 cm/19 3/4 x 13 in
Private Collection
RA 402

Jan Toorop   1858–1928

Born in Java, Toorop trained in Amsterdam. He lived in Brussels during the 1880s, returning to settle permanently in Holland in 1890. The stylistic variety of Toorop's work exemplifies the range of visual alternatives available to him through membership in Les XX, through his travels to London and Paris, and through contact with Dutch art. After absorbing the art of Whistler and Ensor in the mid-1880s, he turned to neo-impressionism in around 1888, and then, without fully rejecting the decorative potential of neo-impressionism, he developed a variety of modes of visual symbolism through access to the work of Gauguin and van Gogh. Toorop was a persistent advocate in Holland of foreign avant-garde art throughout the 1890s and a catalyst in Mondrian's move toward abstraction in about 1908. His own art, however, became increasingly marked by his conversion to Roman Catholicism in 1905.

233   *Annie Hall at Lissadell, Kenley*   1885

Annie Hall in Lissadell, Kenley or *Annie Hall à Lissadell, Kenley*
sdbr. Jan Toorop 28.6.85   99 x 73 cm/39 x 28 3/4 in
Stedelijk Museum, Amsterdam
RA 415

234   *After the Strike*   c. 1888

Na de Werkstaking or *Après la grève*
sbr. Toorop   65 x 76 cm/25 1/2 x 30 in
Rijksmuseum Kröller-Müller, Otterlo, The Netherlands
RA 416

235   *Autumn Landscape in Surrey*   c. 1890

Oude Eiken in Surrey or *Vieux chênes dans le Surrey*
sbr. J Th. Toorop   63 x 76 cm/24 3/4 x 30 in
Stedelijk Museum, Amsterdam, Gift of the Vereeniging tot het vormen van een Openbare Verzameling van Hedendaagse Kunst, 1949
RA 417

235

236

237

236   *The Shell Gatherer*   1891

Schelpenvrissers op het strand or *Le Pêcheur de
coquillages*
sdbl. J Th Toorop 1891   61.5 x 66 cm/24 1/4 x 26 in
Rijksmuseum Kröller-Müller, Otterlo, The Netherlands
RA 418 *(illustrated in color)*

237   *The Young Generation*   1892

La Jeune génération
sdbl. Jan Toorop 1892   96.5 x 110 cm/38 x 43 1/4 in
Museum Boymans-van Beuningen, Rotterdam
RA 420

James Ensor   1860–1949

Apart from brief visits to Brussels, Paris, and London, Ensor spent most of his life in his native town of Ostend. Early in his career he had defied the Brussels art establishment by belonging to a radical political and literary group while still a student at the Brussels Académie (1878–1880). By 1882 he was contributing works to the alternative exhibiting bodies, L'Essor and La Chrysalide, and he was a founding member of Les XX. Concerned that his art should not be merely descriptive, Ensor used in his earlier work a rich technique to evoke mood in his domestic interiors and still lifes. In his later work, he introduced specifically exotic subject matter such as skeletons, masks, and Japanese prints, as an expression of his own alienation from his critics and the public.

238   *Still Life*   c. 1882

Nature morte
sbr. Ensor   80 x 100 cm/31 1/2 x 39 1/4 in
Musée des Beaux-Arts, Liège, Belgium
RA 393

239   *Skeleton Studying Chinoiseries*   1885

Squelette regardant les chinoiseries
sdbl. Ensor 85   99.5 x 64.5 cm/39 3/4 x 25 1/2 in
Collection Julian J. Aberbach
RA 395

240 *The Ray* 1892

La Raie
sdbl. Ensor 92; sbr. Ensor
80 x 100 cm/31 1/2 x 39 1/4 in
Musées Royaux des Beaux-Arts de Belgique, Brussels
RA 396

241 *Masks and Death* 1897

Les Masques et la mort
sdbr. J. Ensor 97   79 x 100 cm/31 x 39 3/4 in
Musée des Beaux-Arts, Liège, Belgium
RA 398

Willem Witsen 1860–1923

A painter and an etcher, Witsen was trained at the
Amsterdam Rijksakademie. He was a founding
member of the Sint Lukas Society in 1880 and became
a prominent figure in Amsterdam artistic circles.
Unlike the more internationally conscious cities of
The Hague and Brussels, Amsterdam fostered a native,
tonal, decorative style of painting, of which Witsen
was a leading exponent. He was a major influence in
Breitner's conversion from the brighter, more garish
palette of the Hague School, after the latter's arrival in
Amsterdam in 1886.

242 *The Oude Schans* c. 1889

De Oude Schans
sbr. Witsen 100 x 129 cm/39 1/2 x 50 3/4 in
Stedelijk Museum, Amsterdam, Gift of the
Vereeniging tot het vormen van een Openbare
Verzameling van Hedendaagse Kunst, 1949
RA 428

Théo van Rysselberghe 1862–1926

Born in Ghent, van Rysselberghe attended the
Académie in Brussels. A founding member of Les XX
in 1883, he became Octave Maus' lieutenant for that
group and, after 1893, for La Libre Esthétique. His
links with London and with Paris (where he settled in
1897) led to the inclusion of British and French
paintings in the exhibitions of these groups. His early
work was indebted to Whistler, but, after seeing works
by Seurat and Signac at Les XX in 1887 and 1888, he
adopted neo-impressionism. Although he shared the
French artists' scientific sources, van Rysselberghe's
variant of neo-impressionism conveys a poetic or
suggestive quality which possibly reflects his
friendship with writers such as Maeterlinck,
Verhaeren, and André Gide.

243   *Portrait of Alice Sèthe*   1888

Portrait d'Alice Sèthe
sdbl. V.R. 1888   194 x 97 cm/76 1/2 x 38 in
Musée du Prieuré, St. Germain-en-Laye, France
RA 408

244   *La Pointe de Per Kiridec*
      (Near Roscoff, Brittany)   1889

      La Pointe de Per Kiridec (près de Roscoff, Bretagne)
      sdbr. 18 TVR 89   68 x 106 cm/26 3/4 x 41 3/4 in
      Rijksmuseum Kröller-Müller, Otterlo, The Netherlands
      RA 409

245   *The Canal in Flanders*   1894

      Le Canal en Flandre
      sdbl. 18 TVR 94   55 x 75 cm/23 1/2 x 31 1/2 in
      Private Collection
      RA 411

Henri van de Velde   1863–1957

Van de Velde trained at the Antwerp Academy and under Carolus-Duran in Paris. His early work reflects the naturalistic tradition of peasant subjects and landscape painting exemplified by Bastien-Lepage, Millet, the Barbizon school, and the impressionists. In 1888, the year he was elected to Les XX, he was converted to neo-impressionism. By about 1891, however, his work became increasingly decorative, and contact with the English Arts and Crafts movement led him to abandon painting for the decorative arts, becoming around 1893 a leading exponent of art nouveau. The design and construction of his own villa at Uccle in 1895 opened the way to numerous international architectural commissions which included the Kunstgewerbeschule at Weimar (1904–1906) and the Rijksmuseum Kröller-Müller at Otterlo (1921–1928).

246   *Bathing Huts on the Beach
at Blankenberghe*   1888

Plage de Blankenberghe avec cabines
ns.   71 x 100 cm/28 x 39 1/2 in
Kunsthaus, Zurich
RA 423

247   *Woman at a Window*   c. 1889

Vrouw hij het raam
ns.   111 x 125 cm/43 3/4 x 49 1/4 in
Koninklijk Museum voor Schone Kunsten, Antwerp,
Belgium
RA 424

248   *The Garden at Calmpthout*   c. 1891

Le Jardin à Calmpthout
ns.   70 x 94.5 cm/27 1/2 x 37 1/4 in
Bayerische Staatsgemäldesammlungen, Munich, West
Germany
RA 425

Johannes Thorn Prikker   1868–1932

Thorn Prikker was trained at the Hague Academy in
1883–1887. His early work was in the realistic style of
the Hague School and of Breitner. Contact with Toorop
after the latter settled in Holland in 1890, together
with a growing interest in fifteenth- and early
sixteenth-century Flemish art, led him toward a
nonnaturalistic style of painting in which outline and
the decorative use of the neo-impressionist technique
were applied to religious and symbolist subject matter.
He collaborated with Henri van de Velde on works of
decorative art during the 1890s and was appointed
Professor at the Krefeld Kunstgewerbeschule in 1904.
He exhibited at Les XX in 1893 and at La Libre
Esthétique in 1898.

249   *The Descent from the Cross*   1892

sbl. J. Thorn Prikker   88 x 147 cm/34 3/4 x 57 3/4 in
Rijksmuseum Kröller-Müller, Otterlo, The Netherlands
RA 413

cat. no. 252

The United States

WANDA CORN AND JOHN WILMERDING

The term "post-impressionism" may not seem apt for American art of the 1880–1906 period. The modern movement in the United States was compressed and confused, unlike that in Europe, where one style flourished for a decade or so, to be supplanted by another. Significant lags separated innovations in Europe from their adoption in the United States, and modern movements seldom crossed the Atlantic in pure or complete form. Impressionism, for instance, though it began in the late 1860s in Europe, did not reach America until the mid–1880s when artists began to study the work of Monet and when the New York public had its first opportunity to see, in 1886, the large exhibition of French impressionist canvases organized by Durand-Ruel. It is difficult to characterize the same decade during which impressionism appeared in this country as also the decade of "post" impressionism. Furthermore, the latter term conjures up an image of a rebellious group of painters, radically redefining the way Americans think of picture-making. Only with the formation of the Stieglitz circle in New York City does this country witness such activity. But that history occurred *after* 1906, the terminus of the exhibition.

From another perspective, however, American painters did share broad artistic and philosophical concerns with their late nineteenth-century European colleagues. Americans *were* post-impressionists in their obsession with surface, their rejection of science and naturalism, and their insistence on art as a reflection of subjective experience.

Before exploring these post-impressionist qualities, we should note the relationship American artists had with Europeans during the period. In general, that relationship was one-sided. Seldom did European artists visit America, but Americans considered study abroad and visits to European museums essential to their training. With one exception, the Americans represented in this exhibition—most of them born in the 1840s and 1850s—had been abroad at least once by the end of the 1880s. Some, like William Chase, went back and forth between Europe and America throughout their lives. Almost every artist studied in a Paris studio: Thomas Eakins with Jean Léon Gérôme; Sargent with Carolus-Duran; Whistler at the Académie Gleyre; Thomas Dewing, Childe Hassam, Willard Metcalf, Cecilia Beaux, Maurice Prendergast, Thomas Anshutz, John Twachtman, and Arthur Mathews at the Académie Julian. Several of these Americans exhibited at the Paris Salon and, on occasion, won medals; many were represented at the Paris expositions and international fairs.

Two Americans stayed abroad and became important members of the European avant-garde. James McNeill Whistler lived in London (and sometimes Paris), while Mary Cassatt lived in Paris and exhibited with the French impressionists. Though they lived in Europe, these two expatriates continued to exert an influence back home. Cassatt advised Americans who were collecting French impressionist paintings, and Whistler embraced an aestheticism which many Americans found an attractive alternative to the ideas of the impressionists. John Singer Sargent, while born in Italy of American parentage, was really an international artist. Trained in France and at home in every major European city, Sargent came to the States periodically to paint portraits and fulfill major mural commissions.

Unlike Cassatt, Whistler, and Sargent, whose careers form an essential part of the history of European modernism, the other Americans in this exhibition contributed to the birth of the modern movement in this country. They returned home to make their reputations and, in some cases, to teach. Though none of them had been in close contact with the truly radical European painters (Gauguin, van Gogh, Cézanne, or Seurat), each returned from Europe with an identity as a "modern" artist—as a rebel and outsider—hostile to academic painting and training and eager to educate the public about the new art. In San Francisco, Arthur Mathews took over the directorship of the local art school, substituting the study of the live model for that of the plaster cast and introducing the new ideas about color and form. In Philadelphia, Thomas Eakins initiated the study of anatomy and the nude model at the Pennsylvania Academy of the Fine Arts, an effort so unpopular with the trustees that he was forced to resign. In New York, Twachtman, Chase, Dewing, Metcalf, and Eakins all taught at the Art Students League, a school organized in 1875 to offer more modern methods of instruction than those of the conservative National Academy of Design. In 1877, many of these same artists were instrumental in forming the Society of American Artists, which offered classes and organized exhibitions outside the control of the Academy. By 1898 ten members of the Society considered it too conservative and "seceded" to form their own group and to hang their work in nonjuried exhibitions. Chase, Dewing, Metcalf, Hassam, and Twachtman all showed with this group. Winslow Homer was invited to join them but politely declined, citing age as his excuse.

Other artists simply retreated from the fray and expressed their outsider status in the way they lived. Homer, for example, left his New York City studio in the early 1880s to live out his bachelor life in a house perched on the cliffs of the untamed Maine seacoast. Albert Pinkham Ryder lived like a hermit in a cluttered, disorderly—indeed, filthy—New York flat. George Inness continued his comfortable and gentlemanly existence but became bitter in his late years and increasingly railed against the insensitive public and unscrupulous dealers.

Such disaffection seems tame compared to Gauguin's attempted suicide, Munch's nervous breakdown, or Lautrec's alcoholism. Indeed the alienation of American post-impressionists appears timid and "puritan" when held up against the more extreme European cases. The same could be said about the look of American canvases when compared to the extraordinary color and formal innovations of French paintings in the 1880s and 1890s. But this should not blind us to some rather extraordinary similarities. While the late nineteenth-century American

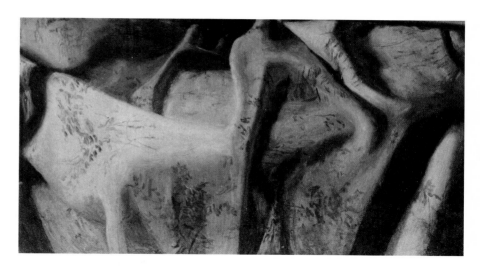

fig. 1 Eakins. *Miss Van Buren.*
The Phillips Collection, Washington.
(detail, cat. no. 260)

painter did not state it with the same flamboyance, he was, nevertheless, as fascinated as his European counterpart with the idea that a painting was *not* a window onto reality but rather a flat surface covered with paint. Hassam's flickering brushwork, Whistler and his followers' liquid veils of paint, Ryder and Homer's crusty layers of pigments, or Sargent and Chase's bravura technique, all manifest the same infatuation with the painted surface. No less than Gauguin, van Gogh, or Cézanne, these Americans wanted us to know that their works were *painted*, not simply copied from nature. Even the late work of Eakins, though considered realistic, calls attention to itself in this new way. There are passages of paint so sketchily applied (the dress of Miss Van Buren, for instance) that we find ourselves marveling as we might with a Sargent or Chase at the beauty of the brushwork while, at the same time, seeing the strokes come together to form a three-dimensional figure in space. (fig. 1)

Like the European post-impressionists, the Americans composed and designed pictures with an eye to abstract design, though never were they willing totally to sacrifice three-dimensional structure and form for flat surfaces of shapes and colors. Perhaps the long-standing tradition of realism in this country prevented their decomposing or flattening the pictorial structure to the same degree as the French. But it is clear that Americans did know about those new ideas, for they had studied Japanese prints, read magazine articles extolling the beauty of pure line and form, and admired the work of Whistler. Their awareness of abstraction shows in their self-conscious silhouetting and massing of forms, their frequent use of patterns, and their calculated asymmetries of composition.

Perhaps the most important similarity between American and European post-impressionism is not stylistic but theoretical. Like the Europeans, American post-impressionists rejected naturalism and attempted to make painting a vehicle for self-expression, for the communication of mood and emotion. When the American landscapist George Inness claimed that art should not depict "an outer fact" but rather "an inner life," he was expressing an international point of view, one shared by almost all of the painters in this exhibition. If Europeans rejected the objectivity and seemingly dispassionate renderings of the realists, including the impressionists, Americans emphatically criticized their own Hudson River school, a group of popular mid-nineteenth-century landscapists whose enormous canvases were microscopic in detail. To the younger generation, these works were anathema, too literal and close to products of the camera's eye.

Though antirealistic and antiscientific, this late nineteenth-century position did not preclude a careful study of nature's forms. Indeed, all of the Americans we are considering worked from factual data, from models, or from landscapes. But they took liberties. They edited and interpreted what they saw to create moods and to convey their subjective experience. No matter how impressionistic Twachtman's palette may appear, for example, the simplicity of the composition, the veiled light, and the hushed quiet of the scene communicate a reverie very different from Monet's work of the eighties. Similarly in Ryder's landscapes— brown and golden restatements of Barbizon works—we find poetry and heightened sensation. Winslow Homer also infused landscape with meaning. His paintings of crashing waves and moonlit landscapes suggest the loneliness and struggle of life. Many late-century Americans, though they may have painted in very different styles, used the same introspective imagery: misty or moonlit landscapes, solitary men or women sunk in reverie, or enclosed, cluttered Victorian interiors. Nurtured in the same intellectual climate which produced Sigmund Freud's theories of the unconscious, these paintings served as metaphors for the artist's growing awareness of his subterranean self. They belong in the same company as van Gogh's emotionally charged canvases and Gauguin's dreamy and mysterious landscapes.

By placing American art next to the work of European masters we can begin to uncover these important parallels and cross-currents, and this is an important lesson of the exhibition. When American painting is studied and exhibited within an international context, the issues of stylistic lags and provinciality become less important. Instead, we appreciate the complexity of cultural relationships. The Atlantic was not just a barrier but a bridge.

George Inness   1825–1894

Inness arrived at his own late personal style principally through the nostalgic romanticism of French Barbizon painting, to which he had been exposed during a series of trips to Europe from the 1850s to the 1870s. Born in Newburgh, New York, he returned from his European visits to paint extensively in the countryside around Boston and New York City. Besides the Barbizon tradition, a second major influence on his later work was the spiritualist writings of Emmanuel Swedenborg, which motivated him from the mid-eighties on to adopt a transcendental vision of nature. He was never really interested in objectively or scientifically recording the transient surface of nature. Impressionism, he declared, was "a mere passing fad," a "sham," and a "pancake of color." Inness cared rather for articulating emotion and spirituality through often gauzy brushwork and evocative color variations. Such a highly subjective approach to working from nature has its analogues in both the classic post-impressionists as well as the contemporary French symbolists.

250   *Overlooking the Hudson at Milton*   1888

sdbr. G. Inness 1888   68.5 x 56 cm/27 x 22 in
Nelson Gallery—Atkins Museum, Kansas City,
Missouri, Nelson Fund

James McNeill Whistler   1834-1903

Whistler, born in Massachusetts, attended West Point Military Academy and worked for the United States Coast and Geodetic Survey before going to France in 1855 to become an artist. In 1856 he studied at the Académie Gleyre. In 1858 he met Fantin-Latour and Courbet and became one of the realist circle. He moved to London in 1859 and spent most of his life there. As his style developed, his work moved increasingly toward abstraction: forms were flattened, settings simplified, color harmonies emphasized, and paint applied in thin layers, creating a hazy, atmospheric effect. In 1877 he exhibited at the opening exhibition of the Grosvenor Gallery; Ruskin, writing about Whistler's *Nocturne in Black and Gold: The Falling Rocket*, accused him of "flinging a pot of paint in the public's face." In response, Whistler brought a lawsuit against the critic and won, although the resultant legal fees bankrupted him. In September 1879 Whistler visited Venice, which proved a potent source of inspiration. He acquired an international following during the 1880s and was elected president of the Royal Society of British Artists in 1886-1888. In 1893 he briefly moved to Paris, then returned to London where he spent the remainder of his life.

251   *The Lagoon, Venice: Nocturne in Blue and Silver*   1879/1880

sbr. with butterfly   51 x 65.5 cm/20 x 25 3/4 in
Museum of Fine Arts, Boston, Emily L. Ainsley Fund

254

255

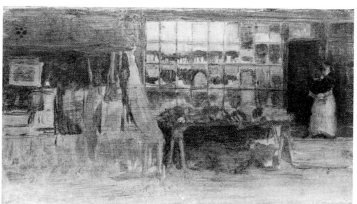

253

252   *Green and Violet, Dieppe*   c. 1885

sbr. with butterfly   oil on panel   12 x 21.5 cm/
5 x 8 1/2 in
Private Collection, Jersey
RA 354

253   *The General Dealer*   c. 1888

sbr and sbl. with butterflies   oil on panel
12.5 x 22 cm/5 x 8 3/4 in
Museum of Art, Rhode Island School of Design,
Providence
RA 355

254   *Mrs. Charles Whibley Reading*   1894

ns.   oil on panel   21.5 x 12.5 cm/8 1/2 x 5 in
Hunterian Art Gallery, University of Glasgow,
Birnie Philip Bequest
RA 356

255   *George W. Vanderbilt*   1897/1898

ns.   208.5 x 91 cm/82 x 36 in
National Gallery of Art, Washington
Gift of Edith Stuyvesant Gerry, 1959

Winslow Homer   1836–1910

Boston-born Homer remained deeply attached
personally and artistically to New England all his life.
Trained as a lithographer and wood engraver, he
brought to his subsequent work in watercolor and oil a
controlling sense of tonal contrast and clearly outlined
form. Two important trips abroad—to Paris in
1867–1868 and to Tynemouth, England in
1881–1882—exposed him to current trends in
European painting. Like many of his contemporaries,
he was influenced by the designs of Japanese prints.
From the mid-eighties on he settled permanently at
Prout's Neck on the rugged Maine coast, with periodic
excursions to the Canadian north woods and to the
Caribbean islands, pursuing adventure as well as
novel subjects. Increasingly after his English trip, he
gave up the anecdotal narratives and youthful themes
of his earlier work for the serious and stark
confrontations of nature's basic elements. In many of
his canvases from the 1890s human figures disappear
almost entirely, as he addressed the mystery and
power of pure natural forces. Paralleling the evolution
of impressionism abroad, his images after 1880 move
beyond the surface recording of casual moments to
compositions of carefully calculated structure,
sensuous deployment of paint and color, and deeply
felt personal visions.

256   *Sunlight on the Coast*   1890

sdbl. Winslow Homer 1890
77 x 123 cm/30 1/4 x 48 1/2 in
The Toledo Museum of Art, Ohio, Gift of Mr. and Mrs.
Edward Drummond Libbey

257   *Sleigh Ride*   c. 1893?

ns.   36 x 51 cm/14 1/4 x 20 in
Sterling and Francine Clark Art Institute,
Williamstown, Massachusetts
(illustrated in color)

Mary Cassatt 1844-1926

Born near Pittsburgh, Cassatt studied art in Philadelphia during 1861-1865, before leaving the United States to travel widely in Europe. She first exhibited at the Salon in 1872 and settled in Paris in 1874, evolving her style through contact with Manet and particularly with Degas, who became a lifelong friend. During this period her paintings were characterized by freely brushed, soft-edged forms, but in the 1880s her drawing became tauter and her forms more crisply silhouetted. Exposure to Japanese prints certainly played a major part in this development, as did her work as a printmaker, for which she used these prints as models. Throughout 1877-1881 she exhibited

with the impressionists, and in the 1890s her work was shown in Durand-Ruel's gallery. Her paintings focused on women and children in interiors, a subject she treated with sympathetic interest. This choice also allowed her to explore her central preoccupation, which, as Degas wrote, was the study of "reflections and shadows on skin and costumes for which she has the greatest feeling and understanding."

258   *Lydia at a Tapestry Loom*   c. 1881

sbr. Mary Cassatt   65.5 x 92 cm/25 3/4 x 36 1/4 in
Flint Institute of Arts, Michigan, Gift of the Whiting Foundation

259   *Young Women Picking Fruit*   1891

sbr. Mary Cassatt   132 x 91.5 cm/52 x 36 in
Museum of Art, Carnegie Institute, Pittsburgh

Thomas Eakins 1844–1916

Born in Philadelphia, Eakins was trained in art at the Pennsylvania Academy and in anatomy at the Jefferson Medical College. After several years of further study in France during the late 1860s, he returned home for the balance of his career, one increasingly embattled, as his direct and probing paintings uncomfortably scrutinized contemporary genteel tastes. Disappointed by critical and popular rejection of his powerful medical-lesson canvases and saddened by the sequential deaths of family members close to him, Eakins turned his attentions more fully in his later career to portraits of single individuals in isolation. Where his outdoor rowing scenes of the seventies might be said to parallel the plein-air subjects of the impressionists, Eakins had all but given up his celebrations of the natural world by the 1880s,

preferring rather to examine the human condition in brooding darkness with tender sympathy and unrelenting honesty. His scientific observation, his classical academic drawing, and his accuracy in delineating the physical human presence in his figure painting from the later eighties onward were above all grounded in a profound psychological truthfulness. In some instances his later portraits possess exquisite treatments of color, either as delicate independent patterns or as compelling agents of emotional feeling. But it is the subjective inner world, consistently embodied in postures and glances of meditation, which firmly places Eakins' mature art in a late nineteenth-century aesthetic.

260   *Miss Van Buren*   c. 1891

    ns.   113 x 81.5 cm/44 1/2 x 32 in
The Phillips Collection, Washington

Albert Pinkham Ryder 1847–1917

The most visionary, even religious, of later
nineteenth-century American artists, Ryder was born
in New Bedford, Massachusetts. Like Herman
Melville, whose novel *Moby Dick* began in that port
city, Ryder grew up conscious of the sea and the coast.
He had poor eyesight from childhood and
consequently tended to see landscapes in broad
masses of shape and light. As he himself later wrote,
"My colors are not those of nature. . . . There was no
detail to vex the eye. Three solid masses of form and
color—sky, foliage, and earth—the whole bathed in an
atmosphere of golden luminosity." Between the late
1870s and late nineties Ryder made several voyages
abroad, not so much to study the old masters in
museums as to experience the sea passage itself and
the sun or moonlight on the water. His earlier works

done around New Bedford and the island of Martha's
Vineyard are glowing pastoral visions, usually with
open fields, a strongly silhouetted tree or two, and a
grazing farm animal. For his later work he drew his
mysterious subjects from the Bible, the tales of
Chaucer and Shakespeare, and romantic poetry. But he
reinterpreted their narrative in subjective, imaginative
terms, stressing the miraculous and spiritual, and
creating abstracted forms, rich impastos, and poetic
rhythms of color. His evocative sequence of moonlight
marines, painted in his last years, provide haunting
parallels to Gauguin's work in their interior vision and
concentration on the formal values of art.

261   *Moonlit Cove*   1880/1890

ns.   35.5 x 43 cm/14 x 17 in
The Phillips Collection, Washington

William Merritt Chase 1849–1916

Chase was born in rural Indiana and grew up in Indianapolis before moving to New York for study in his early twenties. During the mid-1870s he spent several years in Munich, where, along with his fellow students Frank Duveneck and John H. Twachtman, he developed a style of bravura brushwork and rich chiaroscuro effects indebted to seventeenth-century Dutch and Spanish art. In 1878 he began a long teaching career in New York, Philadelphia, and elsewhere. By the early eighties his own painting style began to shift toward the lighter palette of impressionism in response to several factors: his exposure to current French painting, his increasing experimentation with plein-air painting, and his growing interest in the recent works of James Whistler,

whom he finally met in 1885. While some of Chase's later canvases maintain certain aspects associated with earlier impressionism—the light palette, fluid brushwork, and naturalistic vision—equally often his views of the eighties and nineties maintain an alternate interest in solid forms, dense decorative designs, and calculated pictorial structure. His portraits of seated women especially recall Whistler's formal figural arrangements and Japanese prints, notably their silhouettes against plain surfaces and colorful floral patterns.

262   *The Blue Kimono*   c. 1898

sbr. Wm. M. Chase   145 x 113 cm/57 x 44 1/2 in
The Parrish Art Museum, Southampton,
New York, Littlejohn Collection

Thomas Anshutz   1851–1912

Although born in Newport, Kentucky, Anshutz came to be totally identified with the Philadelphia artistic tradition. He was a student of Thomas Eakins at the Pennsylvania Academy in the late 1870s, then his assistant, and finally his successor when Eakins was forced to leave his teaching position in 1886. The younger man continued Eakins' approach, emphasizing the importance of anatomy and of direct sketching from life. Anshutz's paintings, like those of his teacher, were often devoted to single, isolated figures in contemplative poses and painted with warm expressive colors. But also like Eakins, Anshutz painted individuals in a natural stance and environment, notably in one of his best known and most unusual works, *Ironworkers—Noontime*, c. 1882. Its unsentimental observation of everyday social

conditions and careful recording of active figures in bold direct lighting recall Eakins' arcadian themes, now updated to address the themes of labor and industry that came to prominence in later nineteenth-century American and European painting. The subject and its treatment form the foundation for the subsequent work by Robert Henri and the American Ash Can school as well as the documentary photographs taken by Jacob Riis and Lewis Hine just after the turn of the century. The subject has parallels in European post-impressionist paintings by Maximilien Luce and Giuseppe Pellizza da Volpedo.

263   *Ironworkers—Noontime*   1880/1881

sbl. Thos. Anshutz   43 x 61 cm/17 x 24 in
The Fine Arts Museums of San Francisco, Gift of Mr. and Mrs. John D. Rockefeller 3rd

Thomas Wilmer Dewing 1851–1938

A native of Boston, Dewing became one of the cosmopolitan painters of his day, studying for several years in the late 1870s in Paris and in Munich. His earlier work tended to be tightly drawn and composed, yielding in the later eighties and nineties to vaporous effects of brushwork and muted harmonies of pale colors. By the late eighties he had settled on his two favorite themes: one or two women seated in spare interiors, usually playing or listening to a musical instrument, and women poised in the gauzy fields of softly textured and colored landscapes. Both were indebted to the work of his fellow American, James Whistler, and more distantly to the austere interior arrangements of Jan Vermeer. Dewing's hermetic spaces and elegiac tone constitute a central element in American painting at the end of the century; his inclinations to abstracted designs, pure color harmonies, and imaginative reveries have numerous echoes in the work of his contemporaries abroad. By frequently including musical instruments and, equally, treating his color modulations as symphonic variations, he draws attention to the late nineteenth century's fascination with art as music and invites the contemplation of painting's purely formal and subjective elements.

264   *The Letter*   1889

   ns.   oil on panel   51 x 40.5 cm/20 x 16 in
   Canajoharie Library and Art Gallery, New York

John Henry Twachtman   1853–1902

Although Twachtman is perhaps best known for his association with the Ten American Painters and their espousal of an American brand of impressionism, his youthful meeting, in his native Cincinnati, Ohio, with another local artist, Frank Duveneck, was equally important to his career. During the early 1870s Duveneck and William Merritt Chase were working in Germany and had become the dominant American members of the Munich School. Following their lead, Twachtman developed a style of quick brushwork, strong tonal effects, often concentrating on rich dark colors, and broad impasto. But by the 1880s both Chase and Twachtman were lightening their palettes under the influence of French impressionism. Even more decisive for Twachtman was a three-year stay in France and his exposure to Whistler's art.

Twachtman's pastoral landscapes, especially of winter, like Whistler's nocturnes, emerged as evocative and meditative color studies. The paint textures are relatively smooth, the shifting nuances of color delicate, and the often flattened designs recall Japanese prints. Light and diaphanous, Twachtman's landscapes of the late eighties and nineties bypassed the early impressionists' emphasis on the spontaneous moment and uncontrived composition for one of poetic subjectivity, with almost abstract fields of veiled colors.

265   *Along the River, Winter*   c. 1889

sbl. J. H. Twachtman
38.5 x 55 cm/15 1/4 x 21 3/4 in
The High Museum of Art, Atlanta, Georgia,
J. J. Haverty Collection, 1949

Cecilia Beaux   1855–1942

A Philadelphian by birth and early artistic training, Beaux returned from study in Paris in the late 1880s and from 1895 taught at the Pennsylvania Academy until 1915. Her portrait style owed some of its initial stimulus to Whistler's influential 1871 composition of his mother, though much of her mature work is closer to the elegant and dexterous brushwork of John Singer Sargent's fashionable portraiture. While her consciousness of the casual moment and her quick brush in bright colors may be loosely associated with the legacy of impressionism, Beaux's use of solid forms and interest in expressing feeling, even on occasion a certain psychological presence, align more readily with the subsequent artistic concerns of the post-impressionist generation. Through the eighties and nineties she continued to travel in Europe

regularly and became closely associated with colleagues having similar interests, such as William Merritt Chase and Childe Hassam. Beaux's most familiar images join Sargent's in capturing with flattering dash the environment and dress of aristocratic international society in the years around the turn of the century. At the same time there are unusual moments in her work when she exhibits a brooding elegiac mood and a sensitivity to patterns of color for their own formal expressiveness.

266   *Dorothea in the Woods*   1897

sdbl. Cecilia Beaux/97   115.5 x 101.5 cm/
53 1/4 x 40 in
The Whitney Museum of American Art, New York,
Gift of Mr. and Mrs. Raymond J. Horowitz, 1970

John Singer Sargent   1856-1925

Born in Florence of American parents, Sargent studied in Carolus-Duran's atelier between 1874-1879. He first exhibited at the Salon in 1877 and in 1882 first showed in London. In the mid-1880s he moved to England, where he lived for most of his life. His friendship with Monet during the late 1880s is reflected in his impressionistic landscapes, particularly their use of atmospheric color and depiction of water shimmering with reflected light. By the turn of the century, Sargent had become one of the most fashionable portraitists of his day, painting the wealthy and titled in a bravura technique which combined free brushwork with thick impasto. After 1905 Sargent spent most summers on the Continent painting landscapes.

267   *Mrs. Adrian Iselin*   1888

National Gallery of Art, Washington
Gift of Ernest Iselin, 1964   *(not in exhibition)*

268   *A Boating Party*   1889

ns.   88 x 92.5 cm/34 1/2 x 36 1/2 in
Museum of Art, Rhode Island School of Design,
Providence, Gift of Mrs. Houghton P. Metcalf
in memory of her husband, Houghton P. Metcalf
RA 333

Willard Leroy Metcalf 1858–1925

Born near Boston, Metcalf joined many of his fellow Americans in going to the Académie Julian in Paris for study. In the mid-1880s he was among the first of his colleagues to work in Giverny near Monet, adapting aspects of the French master's subject matter and style for use in his own delicate landscapes. At this time he also worked at Grez, painting rather sentimentalized peasant children in soft, evocative landscape settings. These paintings are strikingly close to the influential work of Bastien-Lepage and his English followers such as George Clausen. Metcalf settled for most of his later life in New England,

painting its pastoral scenery and leading an art colony at Old Lyme, Connecticut. Although grounded initially in the loose structure and bright palette of the impressionist technique, he moved in some of his later paintings, like John Twachtman, toward surfaces of more tonal and poetic color harmonies, often with an introspective air pervading the recorded view.

269   *Sunset at Grez*   1885

sdbr. W. L. Metcalf/Paris 1885
85 x 110.5 cm/33 3/4 x 43 1/2 in
Hirshhorn Museum and Sculpture Garden,
Smithsonian Institution, Washington

Frederick Childe Hassam   1859–1935

Usually perceived to be one of the foremost exponents
of the impressionist style in America, Hassam also
modified his later work in ways that went beyond or
even rejected traditional aspects of pure
impressionism. Born near Boston, Massachusetts, he
decided early to be an artist. Becoming a highly
regarded painter in oil as well as watercolor, he also
produced delicate engravings, etchings, and book
illustrations. He did not make his first visit to Europe
until the early 1880s and later that decade spent
several years studying in Paris. His street scenes and
garden vistas thereafter bore the unmistakable stamp
of French precedents, especially their light palette,
broken colors, and floral themes. But due partially to
his American instincts for solid realism, Hassam never
permitted his forms to dissolve totally into fragmented
touches of pure color or objective optical sensations.

Much of his painting from the nineties and after the
turn of the century treated impressionist subjects, with
a consciousness of palpable form in some instances
and a strongly two-dimensional decorative design in
others. Never quite so daring as his European
counterparts of the post-impressionist generation,
such as Bonnard and Vuillard, Hassam nonetheless
moved toward an emphasis on sensuous densities of
paint, patterns of color, and abstract spatial structure
for their own aesthetic expressiveness.

270   *Crystal Palace, Chicago*   1893

  sbl. Childe Hassam   45.5 x 66 cm/18 x 26 in
  Collection Mrs. Norman B. Woolworth, New York

271   *The Room of Flowers*   1894

  ns.   86.5 x 86.5 cm/34 x 34 in
  Collection Arthur G. Altschul (*illustrated in color*)

Maurice Prendergast 1859–1924

Of all the American painters who undertook the practice of various aspects of impressionism and post-impressionism, Prendergast came closest to employing the devices of late nineteenth-century pointillism and divisionism. Born in St. John's, Newfoundland, he came with his family at the age of two to Boston, where he spent much of his life. On half a dozen occasions between the late 1880s and the beginning of World War I, he made brief trips to Europe, painting actively in both Venice and Paris. From Whistler initially, and then later from the nabi painters Bonnard and Vuillard, Prendergast developed a style of intense patterns of color, flattened or cropped perspectives, and striking juxtapositions of forms disparate in scale or location. Increasingly his figures and settings, sky and land, foreground and background became fused into an overall mosaic; his resulting imagery emerged as a highly personal combination of the observed and the imagined. Prendergast was always interested in scenes of parks and carnivals, with a holiday mood of optimism and indulgence. This sensibility is not too distant from the *joie-de-vivre* found in the works of Matisse and the fauves.

272 *Summer in the Park* 1905/1907

> sbr. Prendergast 40 x 52.5 cm/15 3/4 x 20 3/4 in
> Santa Barbara Museum of Art, California, Gift of Mr.
> and Mrs. Sterling Morton

Arthur Frank Mathews 1860–1945

Though born in rural Wisconsin, Mathews moved as a child to Oakland, California, where he remained for most of his life, with the exception of several years spent in Paris during the later 1880s and again in 1898-1899. He had some early training in architectural drawing and later taught design from 1890 to 1906, when he served as director of the California School of Design in San Francisco. He was long associated with the development of the so-called California Decorative Style, loosely comparable to the European Arts and Crafts movement in joining painting with all the decorative arts and in stressing the organic harmonies of line and form. His decorations—furniture, picture frames, and murals—relied on painted floral forms and sinuous patterns of color, elements that also characterized his landscape and figure paintings done around the end of the century. His orchestrated nuances of color recall the subjective world of Gauguin, while his flat serpentine patterns parallel the decorative power of art nouveau and Toulouse-Lautrec. Like Ryder's evocative and abstracted forms, Mathews' imaginative sensibility and indulgence in the aesthetics of shape, line, and tone helped to carry American painting in the last decades of the nineteenth century away from the naturalistic vision of earlier generations.

273   *The Wave*   c. 1900/1906

> ns.   98.5 x 91 cm/38 3/4 x 35 3/4 in
> Oakland Museum, California,
> Gift of the Art Guild of the Oakland Museum
> Association

Chronology

1880

Paris, 5th impressionist group exhibition
Amsterdam, Sint Lucas Society founded
Whistler returns to London from Venice

1881

Paris, 6th impressionist group exhibition
Paris Salon reorganized; annual exhibition now under
   control of artists

1882

Paris, 7th impressionist group exhibition
Paris, first Exposition Internationale at G. Petit's Gallery
   (thereafter annually until 1887; impressionists shown in
   later ones)
The Hague, Art Academy, *French 19th Century Artists*,
   includes Barbizon school painters
London, 13 King Street, St. James', small impressionist
   exhibition organized by Durand-Ruel

1883

Death of Wagner
Death of Manet
Paris, Durand-Ruel mounts series of one-man shows of
   impressionists
Sickert takes Whistler's *Arrangement in Gray and Black No.
   1: the Artist's Mother* to the Paris Salon and visits Degas
London, Dowdeswell Gallery, exhibition of French
   impressionists
Brussels, Les XX founded by O. Maus and twenty Belgian
   artists
Berlin, impressionist exhibition mounted by Fritz Gurlitt

1884

Death of Bastien-Lepage
Paris, Ecole des Beaux-Arts, Manet retrospective exhibition
Brussels, first exhibition of Les XX (thereafter annually until
   1893)

Paris, first and only exhibition of Salon des Indépendants
Paris, first exhibition of jury-free Société des Indépendants
   (no exhibition 1885; annual shows from 1886 onward)

1886

New York City, American Art Association, first major
exhibition of impressionism in America, organized by
Durand-Ruel, includes canvases by Monet, Degas, Manet,
Renoir, Seurat, and Cassatt
Thomas Eakins resigns from the directorship of the
   Pennsylvania Academy of Fine Arts, Philadelphia
Van Gogh arrives in Paris
London, first exhibition of New English Art Club
Paris, 8th and last impressionist group exhibition, includes
   first showing of neo-impressionist paintings, Seurat's
   Grande Jatte among them
London, Whistler elected President of Royal Society of
   British Artists
Gauguin's first visit to Brittany
Paris, symbolist literary manifestos by Moréas and Kahn
   published

1887

Gauguin in Martinique
Brussels, Les XX first includes neo-impressionist paintings,
   by Seurat
Monet visits London for opening of Royal Society of British
   Artists exhibition, where his work is shown

1888

Paris, Eiffel Tower begun, built for 1889 Exposition
   Universelle
Van Gogh leaves Paris for Arles
London, "impressionist clique" gains control of New English
   Art Club
London, Whistler forced to resign as President of Royal
   Society of British Artists
Whistler's "Ten O'Clock" lecture published in London and,

in translation by Mallarmé, in Paris
Gauguin joined by Bernard at Pont-Aven in Brittany
Gauguin briefly joins van Gogh in Arles
Sérusier's *Talisman*, painted under Gauguin's instruction at Pont-Aven in October, leads to foundation of the nabis in winter 1888–1889 by Sérusier, Denis, Bonnard, Ranson, joined 1889 by Vuillard and Roussel
Durand-Ruel opens gallery in New York City

1889

Paris, Exposition Universelle held
London, Goupil Gallery, *Monet* exhibition
Paris, Café Volpini, exhibition of *Groupe impressionniste et synthétiste* mounted by Gauguin and his friends
Amsterdam, first exhibition in Holland of painters of Les XX
Oslo, Munch's first one-man exhibition
Munich, Glaspalast, first exhibition (annually thereafter)
Worpswede artists' colony started by Mackensen, Modersohn, and H. am Ende
London, Goupil Gallery, *London Impressionists* exhibition, with catalogue preface by Sickert

1890

Death of van Gogh
Denis' "Définition du néo-traditionnisme" published
Paris, first exhibition of Société Nationale des Beaux-Arts (founded as alternative to Salon, with Meissonier as president, Puvis de Chavannes as vice-president; thereafter annual shows)
London, New Gallery, first exhibition of Arts and Crafts Exhibition Society
San Francisco, Arthur Mathews appointed director, California School of Design
Livorno, Bagni Pancaldi, Müller exhibits impressionist-influenced works
Florence, impressionist-influenced paintings by Müller, Kienerk, Nomellini shown, exhibition extends into 1891

1891

Death of Seurat
Gauguin leaves for Tahiti
Publication of Péladan's *Salon de la Rose + Croix, règle et monitoire*
Publication of Aurier's "Le Symbolisme en peinture, Paul Gauguin"
Paris, Monet Haystacks series exhibited (his first series)
Milan, first divisionist works shown at Brera Triennale, by Segantini, Previati, Longoni, and probably Morbelli, Grubicy, Nomellini
Saint-Germain-en-Laye, Château, first group exhibition of the nabis
Paris, Le Barc de Boutteville mounts first *Exposition des Peintres Impressionnistes et Symbolistes* (frequent shows until 1897)

1892

Munich Secession founded
Berlin, Gruppe XI founded in protest of Munch's treatment at Association of Berlin Artists exhibition; later forms nucleus of Berlin Secession
Paris, first Salon de la Rose + Croix (annual shows until 1897)
London, Goupil Gallery, *Whistler* retrospective
The Hague, Kunstkring, *Van Gogh* exhibition
The Hague, Kunstkring, exhibition of *Société des XX*

1893

London, Grafton Galleries, inaugural exhibition
Munch comes to Berlin
Paris, Durand-Ruel exhibits Gauguin's Tahitian paintings
Chicago, Columbian Exposition, Mary Cassatt paints mural for the Women's Building

1894

Brussels, first exhibition of La Libre Esthétique, group which replaced Les XX, annual shows thereafter include decorative as well as fine arts
Bremen, Kunsthalle, first group exhibition of Worpswede artists

1895

London, Oscar Wilde trial
Berlin, Ugo Barroccio Gallery, *Munch* exhibition (Love series)
Venice, first Biennale exhibition, international sections do not include French avant-garde painting
Paris, Vollard mounts first Cézanne one-man show
Bing mounts Salon de l'Art Nouveau, including fine and decorative arts

1896

Berlin, von Tschudi becomes director of the National Gallery (until 1908) and encourages acquisition of French works
Florence, Festa dell'Arte e dei Fiori, major international exhibition, extends into spring 1897
New York City, William Merritt Chase founds The Chase School of Art

1897

Paris, part of Caillebotte bequest shown in Musée du Luxembourg
Venice, 2 Monets and a Renoir shown at Biennale
New York City, "Ten American Painters" leave the Society of American Artists to form their own association

1898

Deaths of Moreau, Puvis de Chavannes
New York City, Durand-Ruel Galleries, first exhibition of "The Ten"

Periodical publication of Signac's *D'Eugène Delacroix au néo-impressionnisme* (published in book form, 1899)
London, International Society, first exhibition, with Whistler as president, major showing of recent avant-garde painting

1899

Paris, Durand-Ruel's Galleries, mixed exhibition including Redon, nabis, neo-impressionists
Berlin, first exhibition of newly formed Secession, with Liebermann as president
Death of Segantini

1900

Paris, Exposition Universelle
Picasso first visits Paris

1901

Death of Toulouse-Lautrec
Paris, Bernheim Jeune Gallery mounts *Vincent Van Gogh*, a major exhibition
Munich, first Phalanx exhibition, with Kandinsky as president
The Hague, first International Exhibition

1903

Deaths of Gauguin in Marquesas Islands and Camille Pissarro
Paris, Vollard mounts *Gauguin* exhibition
New York City, *Camera Work* begins publication
Paris, first exhibition of Salon d'Automne (thereafter annually)

1904

Paris, Salon d'Automne includes separate rooms devoted to Cézanne, Puvis de Chavannes, Redon, Renoir, and Toulouse-Lautrec

1905

London, Grafton Galleries, major impressionist exhibition organized by Durand-Ruel
Paris, Indépendants exhibition includes retrospectives of van Gogh and Seurat
New York City, Alfred Stieglitz opens the Photo-Secession Galleries at 291 Fifth Avenue
Amsterdam, Stedelijk Museum, *Van Gogh* exhibition
Dresden, the Brücke group founded by Kirchner and others
Dresden, Galerie Arnold, *Van Gogh* exhibition
Previati publishes *La Technica della Pittura*
Paris, Salon d'Automne includes retrospectives of Ingres and Manet; room of paintings by Matisse and his associates in the exhibition is described as the *cage des fauves* and leads to the christening of the fauve group

1906

Death of Cézanne
Previati publishes *Principi Scientifici del Divisionismo*
Dresden, first exhibition of Die Brücke in Seifert's lighting factory
Paris, Salon d'Automne includes Gauguin retrospective
Bremen, Kunsthalle, exhibition of Worpswede artists

Select Bibliography

GENERAL

Bénédite, L., *Great Painters of the XIXth Century and their Paintings*, London 1910

Čelebonović, A., *The Heyday of Salon Painting*, London 1974

Chicago, Art Institute, *Art Nouveau, France, Belgium*, 1976

Gordon, D. L., *Modern Art Exhibitions*, Munich 1974

Hamilton, G. H., *Painting and Sculpture in Europe, 1880–1940*, London 1967

Herbert, E. W., *The Artist and Social Reform, France and Belgium, 1885–1898*, New Haven 1961

Hoffmann, W., *The Earthly Paradise, Art in the 19th Century*, London 1961

Hofstätter, H. H., *Symbolismus und die Kunst der Jahrhundertende*, Cologne 1965

London, Royal Academy of Arts, *Impressionism, its Masters, its Precursors and its Influence in Britain*, catalogue by J. House, 1974

London, Royal Academy of Arts, *Post-Impressionism, Cross-Currents in European Painting*, catalogue edited by J. House and MA. Stevens, 1979–1980

Madsen, S. T., *Sources of Art Nouveau*, Oslo 1956

Meier-Graefe, J., *Modern Art*, London 1908

Munich, Haus der Kunst, *Weltkulturen und moderne Kunst*, 1974

Muther, R., *The History of Modern Printing*, London 1896, reprinted 1907

New York, Solomon R. Guggenheim Museum, *Neo-Impressionism*, catalogue by R. L. Herbert, 1968

*Paris, Grand Palais, *Le Symbolisme en Europe*, 1976

Philadelphia, Museum of Art, *From Realism to Symbolism, Whistler and his World*, 1971

Rosenblum, R., *Modern Painting and the Northern Romantic Tradition*, London 1975

Stevens, MA., "Post-Impressionist Prints," *Connoisseur*, January 1980

FRANCE

Arts Council of Great Britain, *Post-Impressionist Graphics*, catalogue by MA. Stevens, 1980

*Barr, A. H., *Matisse, His Art and His Public*, New York 1951, and reprinted

Blanche, J. E., *Les Arts plastiques, La IIIe République, de 1870 à nos jours*, Paris 1931

Cézanne, P., *Correspondance*, Paris 1978

*Cleveland, Museum of Art, etc., *Japonisme, Japanese Influence on French Art, 1854–1910*, 1975

Delouche, D., *Peintres de la Bretagne, Découverte d'une province*, Rennes 1977

Denis, M., *Journal*, Paris 1957–1959

—, *Théories, Du Symbolisme au classicisme*, Paris 1964

Doran, P. M., *Conversations avec Cézanne*, Paris 1978

Dujardin, E., "La Revue wagnérienne," *La Revue musicale*, October 1923

*Duthuit, G., *The Fauvist Painters*, New York 1950

Duval, E. L., *Téodor de Wyzéwa, a Critic without a Country*, Geneva and Paris 1961

*Elderfield, J., *The "Wild Beasts," Fauvism and Its Affinities*, New York 1976

Fénéon, F., *Oeuvres plus que complètes*, Paris 1970

Francastel, P., *L'Impressionnisme*, Paris 1937, reprinted 1974

Gauguin, P., *Lettres à sa femme et à ses amis*, Paris 1946

—, *Oviri, Ecrits d'un sauvage*, Paris 1974

Van Gogh, *The Complete Letters of Vincent Van Gogh*, London 1958

*Jaworska, W., *Gauguin et l'école de Pont-Aven*, Paris 1971, English translation 1972

Lehmann, A. G., *The Symbolist Aesthetic in France, 1885–1895*, Oxford 1968

*London, Hayward Gallery, *French Symbolist Painters*, 1972

London, Tate Gallery, *Gauguin and the Pont-Aven Group*, 1966

Løvgren, S., *The Genesis of Modernism*, Stockholm 1959

Matisse, H., *Ecrits et propos sur l'art*, Paris 1972

*Mauner, G., *The Nabis, Their History and Their Art, 1888–1896*, New York and London 1978

*Pincus-Witten, R., *Occult Symbolism in France, Josephin Péladan and the Salons de la Rose + Croix*, New York and London 1976

Pissarro, C., *Lettres à son fils Lucien*, Paris 1950

Redon, O., *Lettres d'Odilon Redon*, Brussels and Paris 1923

—, *A Soi-même*, Paris 1961

*with comprehensive bibliography

*Rewald, J., *The History of Impressionism*, London and New York 1973

*—, *Post-Impressionism*, New York and London 1978

Rey, R., *La Renaissance du sentiment classique*, Paris 1931

Rookmaaker, H. R., *Gauguin and 19th Century Art Theory*, Amsterdam 1972

Roskill, M., *Van Gogh, Gauguin and the Impressionist Circle*, London 1970

Rubin, W., *Cézanne, The Late Work*, New York and London 1978

*Shattuck, R., *The Banquet Years*, London 1959

Signac, P., *D'Eugène Delacroix au néo-impressionnisme*, Paris 1899, reprinted 1964

—, "Extraits du journal inédit," *Gazette des Beaux-Arts*, 36 (1949), 39 (1952), 42 (1953)

Sutter, J., *The Neo-Impressionists*, London 1970

Venturi, L., *Les Archives de l'Impressionnisme*, Paris 1939

Vollard, A., *Souvenirs d'un marchand de tableaux*, Paris 1937

Webster, J. C., "The Technique of Impressionism," *College Art Journal*, November 1944

Woolley, G., *Richard Wagner et le symbolisme français*, Paris 1931

GERMANY, NORWAY, AND SWITZERLAND

*Berend-Corinth, C., *Die Gemälde von Lovis Corinth, Werkcatalog*, Munich 1958

Burger, F., *Cézanne und Hodler*, Munich 1913

Cologne, Wallraf Richartz Museum, *Lovis Corinth: Gemälde, Aquarelle, Zeichnungen und druckgraphische Zyklen*, 1976

Darmstadt, *Ein Dokument Deutscher Kunst 1901–76: Akademie, Sezession, Avant-garde*, 1976

Dresdner, A., *Der Weg der Kunst*, Jena and Leipzig 1904

*Finke, U., *German Painting from Romanticism to Expressionism*, London 1974

Hamann, R., and J. Hermand, *Naturalismus*, Berlin 1968

—, *Stilkunst bis 1900*, Berlin 1968

Langaard, I., *Edvard Munch, modningsär*, Oslo 1960

Perry, G., *Paula Modersohn-Becker: Her Life and Work*, London 1979

Rilke, R. M., *Worpswede Monographie*, Bielefeld and Leipzig 1903

*Selz, P., *Ferdinand Hodler*, Berkeley, University Art Museum 1972

*—, *German Expressionist Painting*, Berkeley 1957

Stuttmann, F., *Max Liebermann*, Hanover 1961

*Voss, H., *Franz von Stuck 1863–1928, Werkcatalog der Gemälde*, Munich 1973

*Washington, National Gallery of Art, *Edvard Munch: Symbols and Images*, 1978 (including essays by R. Rosenblum and A. Eggum)

GREAT BRITAIN

Arts Council of Great Britain, *Decade 1890–1900*, catalogue by A. Bowness and B. Laughton, 1967

*Baron, W., *Sickert*, London 1973

*—, *The Camden Town Group*, London 1979

Bradford, Art Gallery, *Sir William Rothenstein 1872–1945: a centenary exhibition*, 1972

Cooper, D., *The Courtauld Collection*, London 1954

*Farr, D., *English Art 1870–1940*, Oxford 1979

*Irwin, D. and F., *Scottish Painters at Home and Abroad 1700–1900*, London 1975

*Laughton, B., *Philip Wilson Steer*, Oxford 1971

—, "The British and American Contribution to Les XX 1884–1893," *Apollo*, November 1967

London, Fine Art Society, *Sickert*, catalogue by W. Baron, 1973

London, Tate Gallery, *Modern British Paintings, Drawings and Sculpture*, 2 vols, catalogue by M. Chamot, D. Farr, and M. Butlin, 1964

Nicolson, B., "Post Impressionism and Roger Fry," *The Burlington Magazine*, January 1951

Rothenstein, J., *Modern English Painters*, 2 vols, London 1976

Rothenstein, W., *Men and Memories*, London 1931–1932 (revised edn, ed. M. Lago, 1978)

Spalding, F., *Roger Fry: Art and Life*, London 1980

ITALY

Baldini, U., et al., *Pittori Toscani del Novecento*, Florence 1978

Ballo, G., *Preistoria del Futurismo*, Milan 1964

*Barocchi, P., *Testimonianze e Polemiche figurative in Italia dal Divisionismo al Novecento*, Messina and Florence 1974

Bellonzi, F., *Il Divisionismo nella Pittura italiana*, Milan 1967

—, *Architettura, Pittura, Scultura, dal Neoclassicismo al Liberty*, Rome 1978

*Bellonzi, F., and T. Fiori, *Archivi del Divisionismo*, 2 vols, Rome 1968

Caramel, L., and C. Pirovano, *Musei e Gallerie di Milano, Galleria d'Arte Moderna, Padiglione dell'Arte Contemporanea. Raccolta Grassi*, Milan 1973

*—, *Musei e Gallerie di Milano. Galleria d'Arte Moderna. Opere dell'Ottocento*, Milan 1975

Comanducci, A. M., *Dizionario illustrato dei Pittori, Disegnatorie e Incisori italiani*, 5 vols, Milan 1970

Drudi Gambillo, M., and T. Fiori, *Archivi del Futurismo*, Rome 1958 (vol. I), 1962 (vol. 2)

Ferrara, Palazzo dei Diamanti, *Gaetano Previati. Mostra Antologica*, catalogue by P. Bucarelli, F. Bellonzi, M. Calvesi, and R. Barilli, 1969

Grubicy, V., *Tendenze evolutive delle Arti plastiche*, Milan 1891

Hyogo (Japan), Museum of Modern Art, *Giovanni Segantini*, 1978 and subsequently to Milan, Palazzo Permanente, cat. by A. P. Quinsac

Livorno, Villa Fabbricotti, and Florence, Palazzo Strozzi, *Mostra di Plinio Nomellini*, catalogue by C. L. Ragghianti et al., 1966

Longhi, R., preface to J. Rewald's *Storia dell'Impressionismo*, Florence 1949, pp. VII–XXIX

*Maltese, C., *Storia dell'Arte italiana 1785–1943*, Turin 1960

*Milan, Palazzo Permanente, *Mostra del Divisionismo italiano*, catalogue by E. Bairati et al., 1970

—, *Arte e Socialità in Italia dal Realismo al Simbolismo 1865–1915*, 1979

Milan, Palazzo Reale, *Boccioni e il Suo Tempo*, catalogue by G. Ballo, F. Russoli, and L. De Maria, 1973

*Monteverdi, M., *Storia della Pittura italiana dell'Ottocento*, 3 vols, Milan 1975

Pagani, S., *La Pittura lombarda della Scapigliatura*, Milan 1955

*Piceni, E., and M. Monteverdi, *La Pittura Lombarda dell'Ottocento*, Milan 1969

Previati, G., *Principi scientifici del Divisionismo. La Tecnica della Pittura*, Turin 1906

Quinsac, A. P., "Le Divisionnisme en Italie: un Mouvement difficile à cerner," *L'Information de l'Histoire de l'Art*, no. 2, 1969

*—, *La Peinture divisionniste italienne: origines et premiers développements, 1880–1895*, Paris 1972

*—, *Giovanni Segantini, Catalogue Raisonné*. Publication is planned by the Schweizerisches Institut für Kunstwissenschaft by July 1980

Rome, Galleria Nazionale d'Arte Moderna, *Giacomo Balla*, 1971

Venice, XXVI Esposizione internazionale d'Arte, *Il Divisionismo italiano*, introduction by M. Valsecchi, 1952

Venice, Sala Napoleonica, *Primi Espositori di Ca' Pesaro*, catalogue by G. Perocco, 1958

THE LOW COUNTRIES

Braet, H., *L'Accueil fait au Symbolisme en Belgique, 1885–1900*, Brussels 1967

Brussels, Musées Royaux des Beaux-Arts de Belgique, *Le Groupe des XX et son temps*, 1962

—, *Les Jeux de la lumière dans la peinture belge: de Boulenger à Rik Wouters*, 1965

—, *Peintres belges: Lumière française*, 1969

Colmjon, G., *De Haagse School*, Leiden 1950

Gans, L., *Nieuwe Kunst. De Nederlandse bijdrage tot de Art Nouveau*, Utrecht 1966

*Ghent, Museum voor Schone Kunsten, *Rétrospective Théo van Rysselberghe*, 1962

The Hague, Gemeentemuseum, *Licht door Kleur: Nederlandse Luministen*, 1976

—, *Kunstenaren der Idee. Symbolistische Tendensen in Nederland, c. 1880–1930*, 1978

Hammacher, A. M., *Amsterdamsche Impressionisten en hun kring*, Amsterdam 1941

James, M. S., "Mondrian and the Dutch Symbolists," *Art Journal*, no. XXIII, 1963–1964

Joostens, J., "Henry van de Velde en Nederland, 1892–1902, Belgische Art Nouveau en Nederlandse Nieuwe Kunst," *Cahiers Henry van de Velde*, nos 12–13, 1974

Laughton, B., "The British and American Contribution to Les XX, 1884–1893," *Apollo*, November 1967

*Legrand, F.-C., *Symbolism in Belgium*, Brussels 1972

Looijes-Terpstra, A. B., *Moderne Kunst in Nederland 1900–1914*, Utrecht 1959

Mathews, A. J., "*La Wallonie*," *1886–1892: The Symbolist Movement in Belgium*, New York 1947

Maus, M.-O., *Trente années de lutte pour l'art: 1884–1914*, Brussels 1926

Maus, O., Fonds Octave Maus, Bibliothèque Royale, Brussels

Otten, M., *Albert Mockel: Esthétique du Symbolisme*, Brussels 1962

*Paris, Institut Néerlandais, *Jan Toorop, 1858–1928: Impressionniste, Symboliste, Pointilliste*, 1977 (revised, Otterlo, Rijksmuseum Kröller-Müller, *J. Th. Toorop. De Jaren 1885 tot 1910*, 1978–1979)

*Pollak, B., *Het Fin de Siècle in de Nederlandse Schilderkunst. De Symbolistische beweging, 1890–1900*, Utrecht 1955

THE UNITED STATES

Arts Council of Great Britain, *James McNeill Whistler*, catalogue by A. McLaren Young, 1960

Boyle, R. J., *American Impressionism*, Greenwich, Connecticut 1974

Breeskin, A. D., *Mary Cassatt: A Catalogue Raisonné of the Oils, Pastels, Water-Colors and Drawings*, Washington 1970

Cikovsky, N., Jr., *George Inness*, New York 1971

College Park, Maryland, University Art Gallery, *Maurice Prendergast*, catalogue by E. Green, 1976

Goodrich, L., *Winslow Homer*, New York 1944

Hendricks, G., *The Life and Work of Thomas Eakins*, New York 1972

—, *The Life and Work of Winslow Homer*, New York 1979

Hoopes, D. F., *The American Impressionists*, New York 1972

Ireland, L., *The Work of George Inness, An Illustrated Catalogue Raisonné*, Austin, Texas and London 1965

Leeds, Art Galleries, *John Singer Sargent and the Edwardian Age*, catalogue by J. Lomax and R. Ormond, 1979

New York, Grey Art Gallery and Study Center, New York University, *American Imagination and Symbolist Painting*, catalogue by C. Eldredge, 1979

New York, Whitney Museum of American Art, *Turn-of-the Century America: Paintings, Graphics, Photographs, 1890–1910*, catalogue by P. Hills, 1977

Ormond, R. *John Singer Sargent*, New York 1970

Pierce, P. J., *The Ten*, Concord, New Hampshire 1976

San Francisco, Fine Arts Museums, *The Color of Mood: American Tonalism 1880–1910*, catalogue by W. M. Corn, 1972

Schendler, S., *Eakins*, Boston 1967

Taylor, H., *James McNeill Whistler*, London 1978

Wilmerding, J., *Audubon, Homer, Whistler, and 19th Century America*, New York 1972

—, *Winslow Homer*, New York 1972

Acknowledgments

The Selection Committee for the London exhibition, and by extension, the National Gallery of Art, thank the following individuals, in addition to the lenders, who contributed in many different ways to the organization of the exhibition and the preparation of the catalogue *Post-Impressionism: Cross-Currents in European Painting*.

William R. Acquavella
Mme Hélène Adhémar
Dott.ssa Alberici
Ronald Alley
Clément Altarriba
Mlle F. Amanieux
F. X. Amprimoz
Julian Andrews
Mlle M. E. Anquetil
Colin Anson
Jan Askeland
Colette Audibert
Dr Gunter Aust
Richard Auty

Mlle R. Bacou
Signorine Elisa and
 Luce Balla
Dr Wendy Baron
Ilse Bartlett
Timothy Bathurst
Dr F. Baumann
Dr W. A. L. Beeren
Dr W. Bell
Prof. F. Bellonzi
Knut Berg
F. Bergot
Dr T. Berlage
John G. Bernasconi
Miss Valerie Beston
Mrs Robert Bevan
Signora M. V. Biganzoli
 Morbelli
Dr Erica Billeter
Mlle Irène Bizot
Eileen Black
Mme Blatas
Alf Bøe
M. Boisgirard
Luc Boissonas
Dr Gerhard Bott
Richard J. Boyle
Jurgen Brasche
Hugh Brigstocke
J. Carter Brown
Dr David Brown
Miss Lillian Browse
Dr G. Busch

Mme A. Cacan de Bissy
Mme Françoise Cachin
Jean K. Cadogan
Anthea Callen
Julian Campbell
Arch. L. Cambellotti
Dr Peter Cannon-Brookes
Avv. G. Caponetto
André Cariou
Dott. M. Carrà
Bernard Ceysson
Lawrence Chalmers
Bruce W. Chambers
Mme M.-J.
 Chartrain-Hebbelinck
Francis W. Cheetham
Dott.ssa M. Cinotti
Timothy Clifford
Miss Angela Coles
B. Collingwood
 Stevenson
Mlle Isabelle Compin

Frank Constantine
Avv. F. Conti
Lynne Cooke
Jean Coquelet
Nigel Corbally-Stourton
Desmond Corcoran
Signora and Ing. F.
 Cosmelli
Denis Coutagne
Verv. Lili Couvée
Dr Frederick J. Cummings
Ing. Curti
Caroline Cuthbert

William Darby
Carlos Baptista da Silva
Richard Day
Mlle Catherine de Croës
Prof. Giorgio de Marchis
Dominique Denis
Mlle Claire Denis
Gerald Deslandes
Dott. R. de Tieri
Jean Devoisins
E. de Wilde
Anthony d'Offay
Miss Anne Donald
Douglas Druick
Charles Durand-Ruel

Paul Eeckhout
Christoph Eggenberger
John Elderfield
Dr Lindsay Errington

Prof. M. Fagiolo dell'Arco
Everett Fahy
Dennis Farr
Signora and Prof. D.
 Faucci
Dr Walter Feilchenfeldt
Mlle Catherine Ferbos
Avv. F. Ferraris
Wolfgang Fischer
Mme Jacqueline Fontseré
Jean Forneris
Signora
 G. Franchini Severini
A. D. Fraser Jenkins
Dr Heinz Fuchs

Signora Gandini
Dr Kenneth Garlick
Pierre Gaudibert
Dr Gilberte Gepts
Gerhard Gerkens
Oscar Ghez
Miss Teresa Gleadowe
Dr John Golding
Prof Lawrence Gowing,
 ARA
M. and Mme
 Pierre Granville
Dr Lucius Grisebach
Dr Hans Werner Grohn
Gilbert Gruet
E. M. Gruetzner
Mme S. Guillaume
S. Guillouet

Douglas Hall
Michael Hasenclever
A. G. Hatton
Dr John Hayes
Christoph Heilmann
Prof Robert Herbert
Dr J. Heusinger von
 Waldegg
E. V. Hickey
Norman Hirschl
Prof Dr Werner Hofman
Dr Dieter Honisch
John Hoole
Martin Hopkinson
Jill House

Prof Michael Jaffé
Esther Jagger
Dr B. Jansen
C. M. J. Joachimides
Flemming Johansen
Mrs Diana L. Johnson
Phillip Johnston
Joop Joostens
Ellen Joostens
Samuel Josefowitz
Dr Mariette Josephus Jitta
Claudie Judrin

Andrea Kerr
Wolfgang Ketterer
Dott.ssa V. Kienerk
Dr Christian Klemm
Dr Rudolf Koella
Dr Peter Krieger

Mme Geneviève
 Lacambre
Jean Lacambre
Michel Laclotte
Miss Cecily Langdale
Prof. Peter Lasko
P. W. G. Lawson
Thomas P. Lee
Mme
 Francine-Claire
 Legrand
Mme Nadine Lehni
Guido Lenzi
Dr Helmut Leppien
Michael Levey
Dr Simon Levie
W. Liebermann
Marco Livingstone
Gilbert Lloyd
Dr T. Locher
Guy Loudmer
John Lumley

Jeremy Maas
Yves Mabin
Hugh Macandrew
Mrs Margaret MacDonald
Magne Malmanger
Dott. P. Mantura
Jean-Patrice Marandel
Raffaelle Massarotto
François Mathey
Kenneth McConkey
Ian McKenzie Smith
James McLaughlin
Margaret McLeod
James Meldrum

Prof. L. Menegazzi
Rodney Merrington
Dr Franz Meyer
Henry Meyrick-Hughes
Prof. Hamish Miles
Charles Moffatt
John Morgan
Richard Morphet
Dr Dewey F. Mosby
Alain Mousseigne
John Myerscough

Roald Nasgaard
Friedrich Netzel
Dott. A. Nomellini
Signora F. Nomellini
Hans Edvard
 Nørregard-Nielsen
Dott.ssa C. Nuzzi

Elizabeth Ogborn
Avv. Prof.
 Francesco Ogliari
D. Ojalvo
Richard Ormond
Hervé Oursel
Dr R. Oxenaar
Dott. P. Pacini
Jean Paladilhe
Andrew McIntosh Patrick
C. J. Pearson
Dr José de Azeredo
 Perdigão
Prof Guido Perocco
Dr Hans Albert Peters
Prof E. Piceni
Godfrey Pilkington
F. Pomarède
Sir John Pope-Hennessy
C. N. P. Powell
Dott.ssa
 M. Precerutti-Garberi
Dott. Lucio Puttin
Dr E. H. Puvogel

Pierre Quarré

Patrick Ramade
Dr Robert Ratcliffe
Prof. Stephen Rees-Jones
Sir Norman Reid
Prof. John Rewald
Dr Rickmann
Joseph Rishel
Miss Antonia Roberts
Philippe Roberts-Jones
Alexander Robertson
Duncan Robinson
David Robson
Dott. G. Romano
Sergio Romano
Signora M. Romualdi
Mlle Anne Roquebert
Robert Rowe
Angelica Rudenstine
William Rubin
Mr Karl Ruhrberg

Dott. E. Sacerdoti
Françoise Safin-Crahay
Antoine Salomon
Dr. A. Scheidegger

Prof. Dr Ludwig
 Schreiner
Dott.ssa A. Scotti
Dott.ssa R. Maggio Serra
Brian Sewell
Miss Hsio-Yen Shih
Richard Shone
Dr R. Siebelhof
Peyton Skipwith
David Somerset
Claude Souviron
Dr Frances Spalding
Prof. Dr Erich Steingraber
Timothy Stevens
Hugh Stevenson
Quentin Stevenson
Miss Jacqueline Stewart
Michel Strauss
Dr Roy Strong
Dr Charles Stuckey
Martin Summers
Jean Sutherland Boggs
Dr George Szabo

John Tancock
The staff of the
 Tate Gallery Library
Charles Terrasse
W. N. Terry
Eugene V. Thaw
Colin Thompson
Godfrey Thompson
Richard Thomson
Lynne Thornton
Dott.ssa M. Tomea
Nicholas Tooth
Julian Treuherz
Philip Troutman

Dr M. Urban

Dr J. van der Wolk
Auke van der Woud
Dr T. van Velzen
Dott. F. Vercelotti
Marian Verstraeten
Mme Verwimp
Germain Viatte
Jacques Villan
Mlle Vincent
Prof. Dr Paul Vogt
Claudia von Schilling

Leslie Waddington
Victor Waddington
Dr Hugo Wagner
Miss Ethna Waldron
Robert Walker
John Walsh
Geoffrey Watson
Colin Webb
Miss Angela Weight
Claude Whistler
James White
Daniel Wildenstein
Prof. Frank Willett
Arnold Wilson
The staff of the Witt
 Library

Index of Artists

The numbers refer to catalogue entries

Aman-Jean, 95
Angrand, 78
Anquetin, 96
Anshutz, 263

Balla, 226–227
Bastien-Lepage, 40
Beaux, 266
Béraud, 58
Bernard, 133–140
Besnard, 59
Blanche, 97–98
Boccioni, 228
Boldini, 213
Bonnard, 124–131
Braque, 173
Breitner, 229

Carrière, 60
Cassatt, 258–259
Cézanne, 13–21
Chase, 262
Clausen, 191–192
Conder, 211
Corinth, 177–178
Cottet, 102–103
Cross, 80

Dagnan-Bouveret, 62
Degas, 7–9
Denis, 159–164
Derain, 167–170
Dewing, 264

Eakins, 260
Ensor, 238–241

Fantin-Latour, 10–11
Forbes-Robertson, 209
Fry, 210

Gauguin, 41–57
van Gogh, 64–77
Grubicy de Dragon, 214
Guillou, 37

Hassam, 270–271
Heckel, 189
Hodler, 175–176
Homer, 256–257

Inness, 250

Khnopff, 230–232
Kirchner, 187–188

Lacombe, 141
La Touche, 79
Lavery, 193
Lévy-Dhurmer, 113
Liebermann, 174
Luce, 82–83

Maignan, 38
Maillol, 99
Manet, 6
Mathews, 273
Matisse, 153–158
Metcalf, 269
Meyer de Haan, 63
Modersohn, 182
Modersohn-Becker, 185–186
Monet, 22–29
Morbelli, 215–217
Moreau, 2
Moret, 81
Munch, 179–181

Nolde, 183
Nomellini, 221

O'Conor, 199–200
Osborne, 198

Pellizza da Volpedo, 222–225
Picasso, 171–172
Pissarro, C., 3–5
Pissarro, L., 104
Prendergast, 272
Puvis de Chavannes, 1

Ranson, 101
Redon, 30–33
Renoir, 34–36
Roll, 39
Rothenstein, 212
Roussel, K.-X., 132
Roussel, T., 190
Ryder, 261
van Rysselberghe, 243–245

Sargent, 267-268
Schuffenecker, 61
Segantini, 218–220
Sérusier, 114–117
Seurat, 84–94
Sickert, 201–205
Signac, 105–112
Simon, 100
Slevogt, 184
Starr, 194–195
Steer, 206–208
Stott, 196–197

Thorn Prikker, 249
Tissot, 12
Toorop, 233–237
Toulouse-Lautrec, 118–121
Twachtman, 265

Vallotton, 122–123
van de Velde, 246–248
Vlaminck, 165–166
Vuillard, 142–152

Whistler, 251–255
Witsen, 242